Constantine the Great:
Warlord of Rome

Constantine the Great: Warlord of Rome

Elizabeth James

Pen & Sword
MILITARY

First published in Great Britain in 2012 by
PEN & SWORD MILITARY
An imprint of
Pen & Sword Books Ltd
47 Church Street
Barnsley
South Yorkshire
S70 2AS

Copyright © Elizabeth James 2012

ISBN 978-1-84884-118-5

Typeset by Concept, Huddersfield, West Yorkshire.

Printed and bound in England by
CPI Group (UK) Ltd, Croydon, CR0 4YY.

Pen & Sword Books Ltd incorporates the Imprints of Pen & Sword Aviation, Pen &
Sword Family History, Pen & Sword Maritime, Pen & Sword Military, Pen & Sword
Discovery, Wharncliffe Local History, Wharncliffe True Crime, Wharncliffe
Transport, Pen & Sword Select, Pen & Sword Military Classics, Leo Cooper, The
Praetorian Press, Remember When, Seaforth Publishing and Frontline Publishing.

For a complete list of Pen & Sword titles please contact
PEN & SWORD BOOKS LIMITED
47 Church Street, Barnsley, South Yorkshire, S70 2AS, England
E-mail: enquiries@pen-and-sword.co.uk
Website: www.pen-and-sword.co.uk

Contents

List of Plates

Maps

◇306
Eboracum *Constantine*
York   *acclaimed emperor*
Britanniae

Londinium
London   Augusta
Treverorum
306–12 ◇ Trier
*Constantine emperor
of Western provinces*
G a l l i a e

◇312
*Constantine in
Italy; defeats*
at Turin and

Augusta
Augsburg

Lugdunum
Lyon

Burdigala
Bordeaux   **Viennensis**

Aquileia

Tolosa
Toulouse   Arelate   Augusta   Verona
Arles   Taurinorum
Turin   I t a l i a

Caesaragusta
Saragossa   Narbo
Narbonne

H i s p a n i a e   Corsica   Rome

Emerita Augusta
Merida   Tarraco
Tarragona
Toletum
Toledo

Hispalis   *Baleares Insulae*   *Sardinia*
Seville
Gades   Corduba   M a r e   ◇ Oct 31
Cadiz   Carthago   *Constanti*
Nova   *at Milvian*
Tingi   Cartagena   Caesarea   *control of*
Tangier
Cirta   Carthago
Carthage

A f r i c a

N

0   450 kms
0   300 miles

The Roman Empire at the time of Constantine

1/The rise of Constantine, AD 306–24

Roman frontier

Constantine's realm:

306

added 312

added 316

added 324

Constantine's campaigns:

against Maxentius, 212

against Licinius, 316

against Licinius, 324

battle

◊ 316
Constantine defeats Licinius and siezes Balkans

July 324 ◊
Constantine defeats Licinius

Sirmium

Viminacium

Ister *Danube*

Cibalae
Vinkovci

Serdica
Sofia

Moesiae

entum
anto

Thessalonica

Thraciae

Adrianople
Edirne

Heraclia

Cyzicus

Pergamum

axentius
takes
rth Africa

Ephesus

Athenae
Athens

Byzantium
Istanbul

Chrysopolis
Uskudar

Pontus Euxinus

Black Sea

Sinope

Pontica

Ancyra
Ankara

Asiana

Laodicea

Oriens

Tarsus

Antioch

Palmyra

◊ Sept 324
final defeat of Licinius leaves Constantine ruler of whole empire

Crete

Cyprus

Damascus

Tyre

Mediterranean Sea

Cyrene

Alexandria

Memphis

Aegyptus

Nilus
Nile

Hierosolyma
Jerusalem

The Battle of Turin

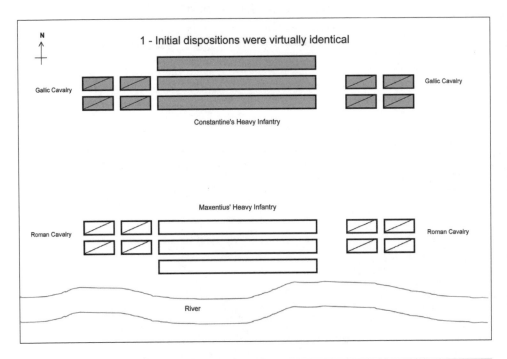

1 - Initial dispositions were virtually identical

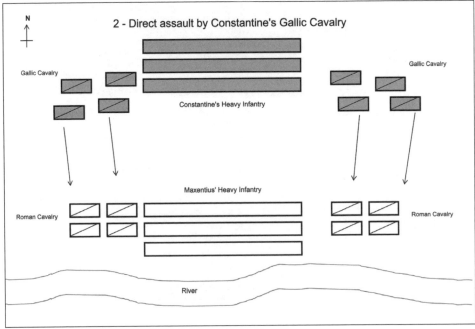

2 - Direct assault by Constantine's Gallic Cavalry

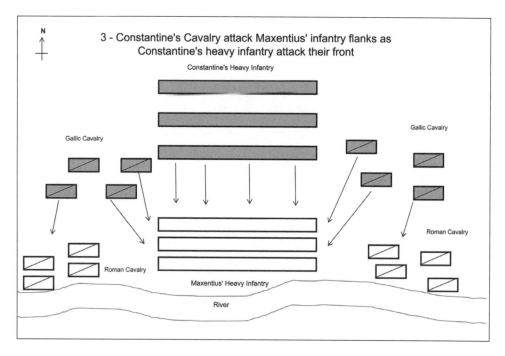

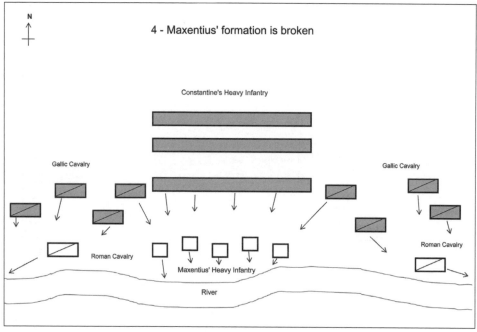

The Battle of the Milvian Bridge

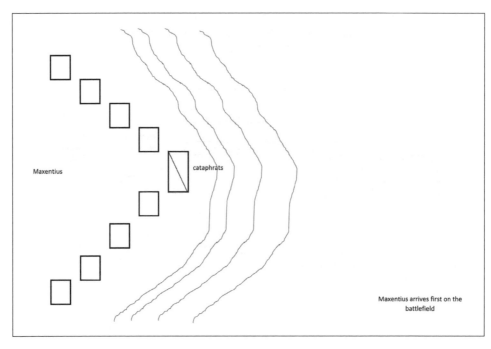

Maxentius

cataphrats

Maxentius arrives first on the battlefield

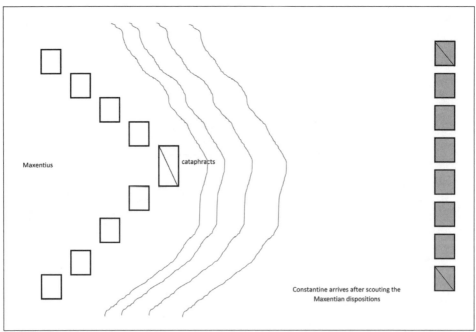

Maxentius

cataphracts

Constantine arrives after scouting the Maxentian dispositions

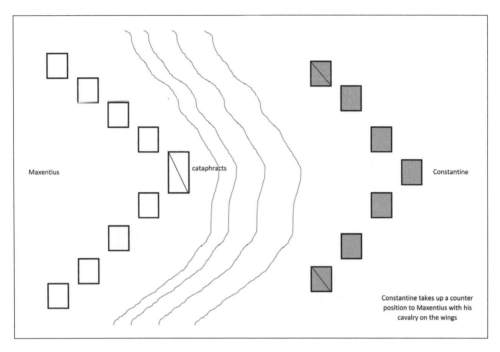

Maxentius

cataphracts

Constantine

Constantine takes up a counter position to Maxentius with his cavalry on the wings

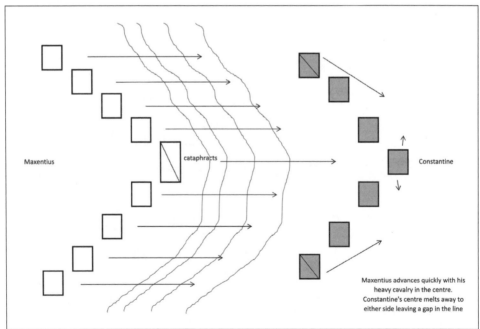

Maxentius

cataphracts

Constantine

Maxentius advances quickly with his heavy cavalry in the centre. Constantine's centre melts away to either side leaving a gap in the line

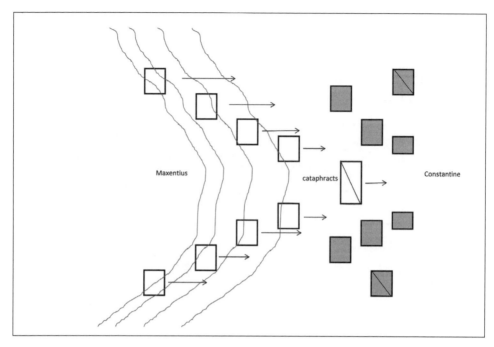

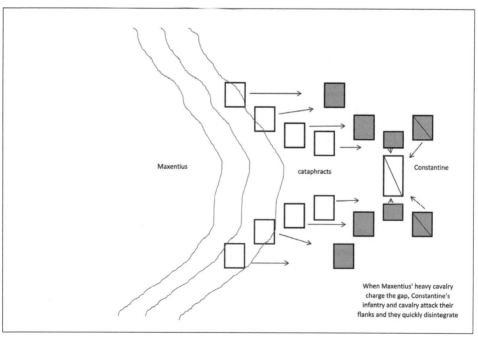

When Maxentius' heavy cavalry charge the gap, Constantine's infantry and cavalry attack their flanks and they quickly disintegrate

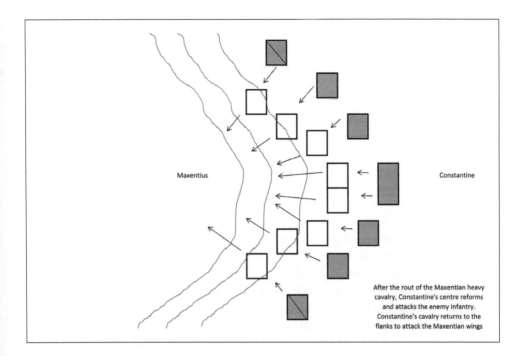

Maxentius

Constantine

After the rout of the Maxentian heavy cavalry, Constantine's centre reforms and attacks the enemy infantry. Constantine's cavalry returns to the flanks to attack the Maxentian wings

Preface

Since the explosion in the popularity of and interest in the world of Late Antiquity, the Transformation of the Roman Empire, and the resultant empire of Byzantium, there have already been very many books written and published on Constantine, his life, his Christianity and his historical context. What then, the case for another? Constantine's life and times have excited particular interest for one inevitable and hugely important reason: his life is inextricably linked to the history of Christianity, and to tell that story fully we needs must look back to this one man whose life achievements were many. In this regard, this life of Constantine is not too different: it is impossible to tell his story without also referring to the Christianity that became such a major part of his life, and to analyse some aspects of his relationship to religion and the growth of the church in the context of his career as statesman and soldier.

Where this life differs from the many already to be found is in its focus on Constantine's military campaigns and successes. What is possible to overlook is the fact that Constantine's career as patron of Christianity, protector of the faith and pivotal role in the development of a new Christian culture was all built on the field of battle. Without his extraordinary success in this respect: his strategy, his fine soldier's instinct, his self-belief and the loyalty he inspired among his troops, then none of his victories would have even taken place. And without those victories, Constantine would never have achieved the power he eventually wielded, and which he used so extensively and creatively to start changing the Roman Empire and shaking it to its very core. To say nothing of the new Christian culture that grew out of Constantine's life and times, the very fact that this was a man who had the sheer confidence, bravado and extraordinary dynamism not only to transfer the imperial capital from Rome, but also to rebuild and refashion the imperial backwater that was Byzantium – and not only that, to rename it

'The City of Constantine' (Constantinopolis/Constantinople) – should remind us what we are dealing with here. We have a man who was, truly, a great man of action: a great Roman emperor. A successful soldier, general and strategist; and perhaps, the very best Roman emperor of them all.

Acknowledgements

My interest in the later Roman Empire and the world of Late Antiquity originates in my undergraduate studies at Cambridge, where I read Classics. Here, the Roman Empire as I had never known it before was opened up for me; and for this I have to thank all the lecturers and tutors at the Classics Faculty who made this so, and all of my contemporaries and associates at this time who encouraged me to think. Intending to take my study of early Christianity further, I applied for the MA in Classics and Theology at Durham, and was among the last of the intake to complete this specialised joint honours degree. At Durham, I deepened my understanding of the New Testament and its textual history, early Christian life and culture and Neoplatonism. The Theology Department at Durham was another wonderful place to study and I thank everyone at Durham University and in Durham University Library (where much of this book was written) for this stimulating learning environment, and especially for the inspirational view of Durham Cathedral to be had from the top floor.

For his patience, understanding and meticulous attention to detail, I have to thank Phil Sidnell at Pen and Sword, without whom this book would never have been written. I also thank everyone at Pen and Sword who has helped bring this book to completion. For lending me very many useful and appropriate books (even his own copy of the Latin Panegyrics) I have to thank Martin Foulkes, and for many interesting conversations about ancient textiles, and in particular weaving (and for lessons on the same) my friend Sue Foulkes who is herself a very talented weaver and who restarted my (currently time-intensive) enthusiasm for textile crafts.

Finally, for all his support during the whole writing process, I have to thank my partner Stephen English most of all, without whom this book would no doubt have taken a great deal longer to complete.

Chapter 1

Introduction

Unlike very many other Roman Emperors, whose contact with the undesirably dreary and rainy imperial backwater of Britannia was minimal, Constantine can be considered a far more integral part of British history. In modern day York, Roman Eboracum, his statue stands outside the glorious York Minster to commemorate the place where Roman history was so decisively made. It was here, in the north of the barbarous and strange country of Britannia, that Constantine was raised to emperor on the battlefield, backed by the loyalty of his father's troops after his death which left the way clear for his son. Given the subsequent events in the life of Constantine, it is small wonder that this statue of Constantine, placed as it is outside York Minster, shows him in reflective and contemplative mood, meditating on the Christianity that was to be such a large part of his success. Unsurprisingly, this statue gives us the Constantine of the Church: the Constantine who died on the date of Pentecost in 337, who was considered uniquely favoured and divinely appointed by many of his contemporaries (Eusebius, his biographer, being prominent among them) and who possibly even thought of himself as a second Christ (his plans for his burial and honours after death included a sarcophagus modelled on that of the Holy Sepulchre, a building intended to be the resting place of Christ and contemporary to Constantine's own building). Indeed, in the Orthodox Church, Constantine is still venerated and honoured as a saint, and in orthodox countries such as Greece, nostalgia for Byzantium and Constantine run high indeed, coupled with a strong sense of loss for the city of Constantinople, no longer Greek-speaking though with much evidence of its Hellenic culture still intact for all to see.

But that is just one Constantine. While the Constantine of the Church reminds us of his pivotal role in the history of Christianity, his piety and sincere relationship with the Christian God and his hugely influential and transformative support and patronage of the church in this regard, there are other faces of Constantine. What the statue outside of York Minster does not show is Constantine the soldier, Constantine the man of action, Constantine the statesman and Constantine the emperor. These other facets or faces of Constantine all interlock, but it is through the lens of Constantine's military career, the successes on which all the others are built, that this history is written.

The military lens is so important because it is one that brings into clear focus the fact that the Roman Empire was built on war. Constant warfare, prowess in battle, military might and strength were essential underpinnings of Rome's great success. Had Rome not been able to command such skilled, disciplined and feared troops, and ones which brought so many territorial gains and strategic victories, there quite simply could not have been a Roman Empire. The idea of Roman expansion and conquest would have fallen at the first hurdle; grandiose ideas all undercut by ineptitude and poor planning and tactical errors. Fortunately for Rome, it was able to rely on its supreme military might and the guarantee of success it brought for a long, long time. However, by Constantine's own time, when he came of age to pursue the career path laid down for him by his father and by his own upbringing, Rome had lived through a period of unrest and turmoil, in contrast to the relative stability, the *pax Romana*, that was the upside of Roman rule. Indeed, so tumultuous and turbulent was the period of 235–284, that it has been termed an age of crisis, and in this vorago the strategic genius of a man such as Constantine was sorely required.

Constantine's early life: the sources

In studying Constantine, the Greek language *Vita Constantini* (trans: the Life of Constantine) by the scholarly Eusebius, bishop of Caesarea (in Palestine) and Constantine's contemporary, is probably among the most important of the primary sources for learning about Constantine's formative years, to say nothing of his later career. However, it is not an unproblematic source: in terms of its historical value, there are a few key points to note. Firstly, it seems most likely that the *Vita Constantini* (by no means the only extant example of Eusebius' work; he was a prolific theologian and historian, and was himself heavily influenced by the Christian apologist Origen) was in fact left incomplete by the time of his death in 339, in which case we cannot be entirely sure what Eusebius intended to be edited, changed or removed in the final version; in other words, we cannot be sure what of the extant content Eusebius himself viewed as mistaken or in need of further addition, or edition.[1]

Secondly, it is certainly necessary to bear in mind the extent to which Eusebius is keen to play up Constantine's glory, his elevated and unique status, and to minimise anything which detracted from that. For example, the Preface to Book 1 of the *Vita Constantini* is on the subject of Constantine's immortality, the next chapter is on God's achievement in Constantine, but then moving to Constantine as superior to other emperors, but with a final note on Eusebius' own purpose and plan (an interesting commentary on Eusebius' own reasons for recording Constantine's life in his history). From this, we learn the following:

> As for me, even though to say anything worthy of the blessedness of the man is beyond my power, while to be silent would be safe and peril-free; yet one must model oneself on the human painter, and dedicate a verbal portrait in memory of the Godbeloved, if only to escape the charge of sloth and idleness. I would be ashamed of myself if I did not put together what I can, little though it be and poor, for the one who out of his extraordinary devotion to God honoured us all.[2]

This really does give us a flavour of Eusebius' central bias and leanings: for him, Constantine was clearly God's elect and he always writes his history with this as his lodestar. As for his reasons for writing the *Vita Constantini*, these are simple. It would be 'edifying' for him to do so, because it occasions him to think and meditate on the works of Constantine, and besides, if the worst of the 'godless tyrants' (emperors such as Nero) have histories written by men in stylish prose, then so much more ought an emperor such as Constantine.[3] Furthermore, Eusebius sees his role as not only to record the deeds and words of Constantine the man loved by God for posterity, but also to record these as a means of 'moral improvement'.[4] Thus, not only is the researching and recording to be an edification for Eusebius, but he anticipates that the resulting history will act as a paradigm, since it will be a 'representation of noble deeds', and so will be 'of practical benefit to well-disposed minds.'[5] It is wise to bear in mind this bias and stated purpose in Eusebius' writing: since he is concerned to present Constantine as a paradigm, he is keen to smooth out any rough corners he might find in his character or in his actions, but for a historian it is good to try and read the 'messiness' back into the glossy account where appropriate.

Besides Eusebius, an important source both for Constantine's personal life and his military career are the *Panegyrici Latini* (trans: the Latin Panegyrics). As a genre, panegyrics were often composed and delivered in great numbers for emperors (and sometimes also for other powerful men, such as literary patrons) throughout the period of the Roman Empire, though we happen to have extant examples that date from the later Roman Empire rather than at any other time in Rome's history, meaning that, as a genre, panegyric has come to be associated with this time in particular. Thus, we have the following panegyrics which are addressed to Constantine in particular (panegyrics are typically untitled, reference to them being made by the first line or by a summary of the content):

- To celebrate the Quinquennalia of Constantine's sons; delivered at Constantinople (AD 361)
- *Gratiarum actio* to Constantine on behalf of Autun for tax relief; delivered at Trier (AD 311)
- Addressed to Constantine on his Quinquennalia at Trier after the death of Maximian (AD 310)
- Epithalamium celebrating the marriage of Constantine to Maximian's daughter Fausta; delivered at Trier (AD 307)
- Panegyric to Constantine on his defeat of Maxentius; Trier (AD 313)

The author of a panegyric, by restriction of the genre, can do little but offer praise and glorification of his subject, and the topic of an emperor's military ability (in Latin: *virtus*) was very much an expected one, thus making it likely that any military information to be found here could lean towards the one-sided.[6] That being said, the panegyrics still have historical value, despite their formulaic content. For example, there are cases where the praise is not so excessive as to ruin the sense of its author also being fair-minded, or others where contrary viewpoints, or information that is not quite so flattering to the subject in question, is still included. For this reason, and for the fact that they do contain much battle information useful for reconstructing Constantine's early life and career, they are included here.[7]

The next source to consider is the Latin language *Anonymus Valesianus* (as its titling suggests, of unknown and uncertain authorship), the first part of which document is known as the *Origo Constantini Imperatoris* (trans: the Lineage of the Emperor Constantine). Obviously it is problematic that little is known of the authorship and origins of this source (though it has been dated to circa 340–390, but any more specific date is harder to pin down), since it therefore makes it very difficult indeed to ascertain its historical value, but nevertheless it cannot be ignored precisely because it does give us an account of Constantine's early years. This is not the only reason why it is important not to exclude it: compared to the other two primary sources discussed above (the *Vita Constantini* and the *Panegyrici Latini*) it is exempt from the tendency to an excessive, overt bias that, for differing reasons, characterise both those two sources.

Lastly, and again contrasting against the first two sources that both run the risk of offering only fulsome praise to Constantine, we have the defiantly anti-Constantine, anti-Christian, pagan historian Zosimus, whose Greek language

Nea Historia (trans: New History) is our next important primary source. We know very little about Zosimus the man, such as his place or date of birth, but we do know from a ninth century man of letters that Zosimus mainly relied on Eunapius, whom he is said to have copied from extensively. What Zosimus tells us about his own goals as a historian is also a little limited and unclear; he states that he sees a period of roughly fifty years from around the late fourth century to 410 (the year of the sack of Rome, and an entirely unforgettable date for anyone around at the time or afterwards) as being the one in which things fell apart, where the Romans managed to lose the empire 'by their own crimes'.[8] In which case, counting back from 410, we arrive at a date roughly around 360. What makes 360 notable as a date is that it ties in with the reign of Julian, the pagan blip on an otherwise unblemished record of Christian emperors post-Constantine. But if this is the case, then it is certainly unclear indeed how Constantine (definitely predating Julian, after all) fits in with this narrative of collapse and the undoing of the Roman Empire.

Furthermore, Zosimus himself seems to have something of an internal intellectual division: although a self-designated historian, keen to record important events as he sees them (and implicit in this is the understanding that human affairs have causality) he yet has a strong belief in fate and thus in the lack of personal, individual or human control over events. For example:

> Now no-one will attribute all this [the Romans' sudden and meteoric rise to prominence] to mere human strength. It must have been the necessity of Fate, or revolutions of the stars, or the will of the gods which favours our actions if they are just. Such actions impose a 'series of causes' on future events so that they must turn out in a certain way, and make intelligent men realise that the management of human affairs has been entrusted to some divine providence ... I must, however, demonstrate the truth of what I say from events themselves.[9]

This leads us to speculate how Zosimus internally reconciles the 'point' of history (that is, to explain human events through human, rather than divine, causality) with this tendency towards fatalism.[10] Nevertheless, Zosimus is an important remedy to the praise of the panegyricists and the hagiographical designs of Eusebius, and thus is also a source historians cannot ignore.

Constantine's family

In the *Vita Constantini*, Constantine's family background, starting with Constantine's father Constantius, is understood by Eusebius as a means to explain Constantine's own merit. Eusebius therefore reads Constantius as a god-fearing man also, in stark comparison to the other three members of the Tetrarchy. While it is not too hard to see what the aim of Eusebius' rhetoric is, it does read as a little unlikely. An example of this glorification of Constantine's family:

> When four men shared power in the Roman Empire, this man
> [Constantius] was the only one who adopted an independent policy
> and was on friendly terms with the God over all. They besieged
> and ravaged the churches of God and demolished them from top to
> bottom, removing the houses of prayer right to their foundations;
> he kept his hands clean of their sacrilegious impiety and did not
> resemble them at all.[11]

Eusebius' authorial aim is made manifest. Constantine was a glorious follower of God and founder of the faith; because this was so his father was also a righteous man. But Eusebius' rhetorical goals aside, what do we actually know about Constantine's parents?

Despite Eusebius' best efforts at playing up Constantine's background, especially the piety of his father, it is hard to escape the fact that in reality it was not all that noble or auspicious. Constantine's father, Constantius Chlorus, was an Illyrian soldier from around the region of Naissus (most likely Constantine's birthplace). He was a good soldier and had some campaign success in Britain (crushing a revolt against Roman rule there) but was certainly not an aristocrat by any stretch of the imagination, nor was he a cultured man of letters. Having said that, he is also alleged to have had some interest in philosophy, and it seems that monotheism as a concept attracted him. Perhaps, in common with many other Roman soldiers, he had dealings with the cult of Mithras, and there are some overlaps between this and Christianity; enough for him to be able to think himself around to Christianity, though this is speculation.[12] However, this possible sympathy to Christianity, or Christian leanings, clearly provided enough material for Eusebius to be able to write up Constantius as a full Christian, as the quote above makes clear.

With regards to Christianity, Constantine's mother Helena is rather different, although with regard to her status and background, she did share a little with Constantius. She was from a fairly ignominious background, a low-status young woman whose alleged occupation of *stabularia* (from the Latin root word *stabulum*: tavern or inn) probably best translates as 'tavern woman' or 'barmaid' or 'guest-house owner'; though possibly there is some implication that this '*stabulum*', a word with very low connotations, could also be translated as 'brothel'. If this were the case, it would naturally alter our understanding of the occupation of '*stabularia*' in this particular context, though again, this is speculative.[13] Whatever Helena's actual occupation, there can be no doubt that she came from a low-status background. As a young woman in the Roman Empire of child-bearing age and of limited status, she was also in the 'target demographic' for Christian conversion.

Besides questions of meaning and etymology, there is more reason to think, from the original sources, and from what we know about the harsh realities of the Roman Empire, that Constantius and Helena were not married at the time of Constantine's conception, and so Constantine was illegitimate. From the *Origo*:

> Constantius, a grand-nephew of the divine Claudius [Gothicus] the best of princes, through his brother first became protector, then tribune, and finally governor of the Dalmatians. Then he was made Caesar by Diocletian alongside Galerius. For having left Helena his previous wife, he married Theodora, daughter of Maximianus, by whom he then had six children, who were the brothers of Constantine.[14]

Speculation that Constantine was illegitimate is based on the following: Constantius was a higher-ranking, free-born Roman (in his position as an officer in the Roman army) and Helena was certainly not high-ranking socially, so this may well have made it harder for them to marry, or perhaps even unlawful in and of itself. Furthermore, although Helena is referred to as an *uxor* (trans: lawful wife) or *coniunx* (trans: consort, spouse) in the epigraphical tradition, and there are historians who follow the implication of this and read Constantine as legitimate, there are other references to her status that are less flattering.[15] For example, the *Origo* uses the damning superlative adjective *vilissima* (trans: most base, most vile, most dishonourable) to describe her with regards to her family background, which certainly fits with her class origins and occupation if Ambrose is to be believed.[16] Zosimus, given his bias, reliably accords with this by calling Constantine 'a son of a harlot', and the term *concubine*, which very much does not mean a lawful wife, is also used to describe Helena's status, though the practice of keeping concubines was certainly not uncommon among high-ranking military men who needed to father a son and preferred not to go to the trouble of remarrying, for whatever reason.[17]

Moreover, as the *Origo* suggests, and as is still a matter of much historical debate, Helena and Constantius' union seems to have been somewhat brief, from which we can infer that it is possible they were never married in the first place, since Constantius moved on to a far more august marriage in the form of Theodora. Thus, the charge that Constantine was illegitimate certainly carries some weight, though naturally this is something that historians who wish to elevate Constantine for whatever reasons of their own either try to gloss over or brush out entirely. (As a corollary, it is important to recognise that the family connection to Claudius II Gothicus is entirely false and is simply another example of genealogical propaganda, or wishful thinking.)

Among the historians, the continuing debate over the marriage (or not) of Constantine's parents is made murkier still by the unclear dating of the following marriage between Theodora and Constantius. The proposed date of 293 for the marriage of Constantius (and also for that of his fellow Caesar, Galerius) is not now considered to be all that possible, and the actual date for Constantius' marriage is to be a few years earlier. The historical source evidence for this is convoluted to say the least, but it would seem that the marriages of both Galerius and Constantius did come before their promotion to high rank, but that having this kind of connection to the purple still brought with it the possibility of advantage.

Theodora was the step-daughter of Maximian (in Latin: *privigna* rather than *filia* – daughter – though it is possible she could have actually been the latter rather than the former), and clearly this was more auspicious for Constantius since Theodora was of a better background than Helena. As the *Origo* also notes, the young Theodora proved herself to be an ideal Roman wife, to say nothing of her family connections: she gave birth to six children, and she was most likely only around age seventeen when she started doing this.

Meanwhile, Helena was not exactly forgotten, though she was out of the way with her son Constantine, both in Nicomedia, where they were dispatched and where he grew up. In this time, Helena probably became a Christian convert; a decisive occurrence which if indeed the case would prove to be formative on Constantine's own upbringing, his early years and thus his subsequent military career.

Women and Christianity

What is the evidence that Helena's conversion may have predated Constantine's? There are some Roman sociological realities to consider; Helena fell into the ideal target demographic for Christian conversion, and some examination of the reasons why are worth delving into here. Firstly, the most important factor is certainly gender. Although there are no hard and fast census data to validate this proposition, it was women who made up the majority of Christian converts in the early Church, and they were certainly crucial in the spread of Christianity, from family member to family member.[18] Indeed, early detractors of Christianity before Constantine's time pointed to this fact as supporting evidence for the inferiority of Christian doctrine and practice. It was an old piece of Greco-Roman misogyny to portray women as more credulous or less rational than men. For example, the pagan firebrand Celsus, quoted by the Christian apologist Origen in the *Contra Celsus* writes:

> By the fact that they themselves [Christians] admit that these people [any member of an out-group] are worthy of the God, they show that they want and are able to convince only the foolish, dishonourable and stupid, and only slaves, women and little children.[19]

What is notable here from the remainder of Celsus' work (if we remove the invective) is the interesting insight that Christianity primarily appealed to those of low status in the later Roman Empire: slaves, low-born men or those outcast from conventional Roman society, and women. We could compare Christianity against the military in this regard; as will be discussed, the military also functioned as a lever of social mobility for talented men who otherwise lacked the family connections to make it in society; early Christianity has a little of this quality in that it potentially offered something important to those (such as slaves, low-born men and women) otherwise excluded from wider social participation; the appeal of a belief system that does indeed teach that 'The Kingdom of God is within you' becomes easy to understand for those whose lives otherwise consisted of being at the bottom of the Roman heap.[20]

While this insight is far from original, there are those historians who tend not to appreciate the full force of its implications.[21] In this context, Christianity offered something very powerful; there are the indications that women could gain a great deal of power and influence in the early Church (though naturally this was still problematic for many male believers), and partly came to Christianity for this potentially more egalitarian belief system.[22] For women's status in the early Church, there is evidence that they were important, could preach, make strategic decisions and attain the role of deacon or apostle, and there is good reason to think that many women could enjoy this kind of elevation and accord in the early Church.[23] For an intelligent woman, more often than not denied an education or the chance to exercise their intelligence, the early Church may well have, despite scriptural androcentric bias, seemed like a haven.[24]

Helena, mother of Constantine

This is the kind of social context in which we need to place Helena, the mother of Constantine. As a low-status woman who perhaps found something that spoke to her deeply in the Christian message well before Constantine's own field-of-battle conversion, she was neither credulous nor unreasoned, nor was she doing anything all that surprising, and it seems that in some early Christian communities at least women could find legitimate exercise for their intellectual gifts in the form of teaching, evangelising, prophesying, discipleship or in roles related to church administration and organisation.[25]

Although there is no exact date to Helena's own conversion, it is hard to believe that it would not have been formative. If, for example, Helena did convert when Constantine was much older, in his late adolescence, there is still reason to suppose that this would have impacted on Constantine given that they were not estranged. And if Helena converted to Christianity when Constantine was a much younger boy, then it is even harder to think that this would not have influenced him.

Constantine and his father

Constantine's relationship with his mother, the circumstances of his up-bringing and more importantly possibly even her providing him with his first actual introduction to the Christian faith, was therefore instrumental to his later career and military success. This is no less the case when considering his relationship with his father. Socially speaking, Constantius was a soldier rather than a polished aristocrat. He was not an especially refined or educated man; this was not where his talent lay. Where he did excel was on the battlefield, and in proving his worth as a leader of men and a fighter. If Helena's Christianity possibly informally shaped Constantine, then having his father as a role model must have also inspired and encouraged the young Constantine, not least because his father ascended to the very heights of power in the Roman Empire. As the Panegyricist in his flattering way has it:

> For not only is the appearance of your father seen in you Constantine, but also his temperance, his bravery, his justice, and his wisdom.[26]

It is telling of the social mobility possible in the Roman empire of the time, that a man such as Constantius could actually become Caesar, and that a son of his, born to a waitress, barmaid or tavern-woman, and not only that but a woman who was possibly not even his lawful wife, could go on to rule the Roman Empire and shape the course of events in the way that he did.

However, Constantine's youthful contact was largely with his mother, rather than his father. With Helena despatched so Constantius could make his way, Constantine did not see all that much of his father for the twelve year period from 293 (when Constantine was by this time a young man) and the establishment of the First Tetrarchy. Although Theodora did dutifully bear Constantius six children, the hopes of a dynastic successor still rested on Constantine because Theodora's sons were so much younger when Constantius was looking around for an heir. Constantine was therefore the great hope to carry on the rule, and on him all expectations were pinned. By the year 305, Constantine was in his early thirties, and had proved his military mettle in his twenties, following his father's lead and connections. He was hungry to become Caesar, he knew that he had the military background and capability necessary to do so, and was familiar with the ways of power brokerage in the Roman Empire. He was under no illusions that should Constantius somehow fail or fall out of favour in the west, then he himself, as his son, was also in mortal peril. He therefore knew well that his competence and excellence as a military man were going to be the bedrock of his success; without these, he would have very little to fall back on should the worst happen (Constantius' falling from grace) and certainly nothing at all should he find himself in the even more fortuitous position of being able to order events and seize power for himself.

The Greco-Roman context

Although the events surrounding Constantine's famous conversion to Christianity is the topic of later discussion, since it had such a major impact on Constantine's military career, it deserves some grounding here in religious and social history in order to make it explicable. For example, it certainly wouldn't have been all that obvious to the average non-Christian member of the Roman Empire before Constantine's conversion that Christianity, despite its successes over the previous three centuries, would achieve anything like the ascendency that it eventually did. Indeed, Christianity had already incurred the wrath of the Roman Empire in the form of a series of state-led persecutions that were intended to drive the relatively new cult out of the religious context, though as so often with such overt expressions of state intolerance, these only succeeded in doing the opposite: in popularising and extending the reach of the Christian message by notoriety. There's no such thing as bad publicity, after all.[27]

Therefore, Christianity needs to be set against the set of belief systems usually termed 'paganism' in the Roman Empire, which were very different both to early Christianity and the Christianity post-Constantine. What is most notable is the sheer diversity of Greco-Roman paganism in the first to third centuries. Paganism (from the Latin *pagus*: a village or country district, reminding us of its essentially rural heritage, a bricolage of the folk beliefs of the various groups who lived in Italy before Rome and Roman culture came to dominate) was a broad church indeed, and one that sheltered a great number of cults, deities, public or private forms of worship, philosophies, magical practices and other religious expressions.[28]

Indeed, the official state cult of homage and worship of the living emperor, his dead ancestors and the Greco-Roman pantheon (to which it was expected that all Roman citizens would at least pay lip service) was in fact just one of many possible varieties of Greco-Roman paganism. Besides the officially-sanctioned forms of worship to which every good Roman citizen was expected to pay obeisance, there were curse practices and magical traditions (such as the *defixiones* or curse-tablets commonly found in wells or watercourses in which citizens stated their desires for, variously, revenge, healing, help finding a lost item or sexual conquest), enticing foreign cults from exotic locations such as Egypt, which attracted many with their sheer crowd-pleasing show-manship, carnival atmosphere and occult air of mystique reserved for those initiated into the mysteries (such as the worship of Isis and the secret cult or mysteries of Isis, accessible only to those initiated), or belief systems grounded in interpretations of Platonic philosophy, which attracted those with education who required a world view or religious outlook which could satisfy their intellects.[29]

In many ways, the influx of new and enticing cults from the east made ready the ground for the rise of Christianity, itself at one time a new and unusual cult from the eastern parts of the Roman Empire that took a while before it found high-level and official favour.

Mithraism

Considering religion and the military, the cult of Mithraism, in worship of the god Mithras, had special popularity with soldiers, as well as with those who came from a background of slavery. Gradation, hierarchy and strict pro-gression through the ranks of initiation provided a solid religious structure that proved successful, and perhaps to those used to living with an iron-rule of discipline and obedience (whether to a *dux* or *dominus*) it made sense to transfer a little of this to a religious context, besides the fact that Mithraism was largely a male preserve with appeal to men far more so than women. We can still find some parallels between Mithraism and early Christianity: like early Christianity, which largely appealed primarily to members of out-groups, Mithraism too was a niche belief with particular and specific appeal to certain demographics. Also like early Christianity, Mithraism started life as a small and marginal cult belief-set and then gained ground and popularity over the course of the first two centuries AD. However, unlike Christianity, Mithraism was able to fit into the traditional Greco-Roman pagan paradigm with relative ease since it did not seriously challenge state-power, and was not the subject of targeted persecution in the way that Christianity was. Interestingly, by the time of the Christian ascendency in the third to fourth centuries, Christianity had absorbed some of the symbols and imagery of

Mithraism, such as the *crux gammata*, which reminds us that Christianity successfully took in and then completely transformed pagan ideas and symbols by investing them with its own belief system.[30]

Neoplatonism

If the popular religious current was towards magical practices for everyday complaints and ailments; large and carnivalesque processions and flamboyant festivities; emperor worship and dutiful obeisance to the traditional Greco-Roman pantheon and specialised deities and cults reflective of one's own profession, status or tastes, all of which influenced emergent Christianity in their own way, then the highbrow, intellectual trends to be found in Greco-Roman paganism in the first three centuries were no less influential. But what were those intellectual trends? The strongest and the one which most obviously influenced later Christian theology and thinking came from the stable of Greek philosophy: Neoplatonism.

Neoplatonism is the name given to the evolution and development of Platonic philosophy and practice that came about in the Roman Empire, and was especially prolific in the first two centuries AD, running parallel to the development and spread of Christianity in this regard. The Neoplatonic school was made up of various different learned men (and unusually for the time, even women, such as the Neoplatonic philosopher Hypatia who was brutally killed by an angry Christian mob in the early-fifth century), but most famous and most notable of them all was Plotinus, who is largely credited with a full and thorough reworking of Platonism in his seminal work, the *Enneads*. He lectured and taught philosophy in Rome in the time of the emperor Gallienus, and numbered among his disciples and followers Porphyry of Tyre, who wrote the *Life of Plotinus*, and on which we base much of our knowledge of the man.

Like many other Neoplatonists, Porphyry found the Christianity of his time rather alien and distasteful, even going so far as to publish an anti-Christian tract, and in common with many of his fellow Neoplatonists, he threw the damning charge of atheism at the feet of Christianity. But in contrast, educated Christian men of the second, third and fourth centuries (and beyond) found Neoplatonic terminology, ideas and ways of under-standing highly useful and stimulating for their own thought. Many notable Christian writers and thinkers from both the western Latin and eastern Greek traditions, numbering such luminaries as Saint Augustine, Gregory of Nyssa, Gregory of Nazianzus, Saint Jerome, Origen and Dio Chrysostom, were all heavily influenced by Neoplatonic writings and ideas, and used them to formulate Christian ones on important topics such as the nature and concept of the soul; kingship; the nature and concept of God; and the relationship between the material and spiritual realms. When Constantine himself finally came into contact with the Christian intellectual tradition, he was being schooled and educated in a Christian discourse that owed a significant debt to pagan intellectual culture, in particular Neoplatonism.

Constantine and the transformation of the Roman Empire

In order to understand Constantine's military career, the vast religious and social changes that were sweeping through the Roman Empire before, during and after Constantine's time (a small flavour of which has been given) provide the backdrop. It is hard to write his military history without referring to those other wider trends, in which Constantine had his own substantial role to play, since they help us to understand how power was structured in the Roman Empire. These transformations were those that changed both Christianity and the Roman Empire itself; Christianity transformed from a marginal and persecuted, little-understood minor religion to a powerful, state-backed official one. Moreover, the easy relationship that had existed between the Roman state and Roman officially-sanctioned paganism was broken and transformed completely. No longer the official cult of emperor worship and homage to the Greco-Roman gods; in its place a specific brand of Judaic monotheism: Christianity.

From this overview of some of the wider social trends and power structures in the Roman empire before Constantine, such as paganism, Christianity, social mobility and gender roles, all of which in their own way informed Constantine and shaped his military career, we now turn to one social structure in particular that was most certainly instrumental in his military success: the Roman army.

Chapter 2

The Army: The Social Context

The foreign and civil wars fought between the late third and mid-fourth centuries were constant, and ensured that the Roman army saw near continuous action. Necessity being the mother of invention, the Roman army was thereby impelled both to evolve and to adapt in order to accommodate these stringent demands. In the early part of the fourth century, the empire saw a rapid turnover of emperors, each of whom commanded at least a part of the army. Naturally each emperor also recruited troops, and no doubt paid their own bonuses, to guarantee some kind of personal loyalty as a form of insurance in a world of shifting loyalties and rapid change. Such frequent about-turns of leadership meant that the army was not a simple solid entity, as it was in the Republican and early Imperial periods, but rather a patchwork of sometime cooperative, otherwise hostile, units. It is very important to bear this in mind in order to come to an understanding of the dynamics of Constantine's military career.

However, this is not to suggest that this change in how the Roman army operated was entirely sudden or unprecedented. In fact, since the end of the Republic the army had been subject to massive changes; it was these changes that had accelerated during the third century crisis to shape the army as Constantine and his predecessors knew it. As a result, the army that emerged after the third century crisis, and thus the one that Constantine inherited to command, would have been almost unrecognisable from that of the time of Caesar.

The army: the bigger picture

As the tentacles of empire extended their reach, the army followed and so gradually moved towards the frontiers where the key strategy and territory battles were being fought. Inevitably, this removed the army from the social, cultural and political centre of power: Rome. Traditionally, recruits to the army had been drawn from the many diverse peoples of the empire, but as the army moved away from the centre of power and thus created its own new centres of gravity *in vacuo*, it came to rely increasingly on local recruitment from the peoples of the provinces where it was stationed to maintain numbers. As this process became more commonplace, it caused the links between the army and Rome to be reduced, and ultimately severed. The army of the beginning of the third century would have been largely the same as that of the beginning of the empire, though the powerful social and cultural historical forces were already shaping the army to bring about the markedly different entity that was the reality by the beginning of the fourth. The increase in provincial recruitment meant that by the career of Constantine, most Roman soldiers had likely never even visited Rome.

During the Republican and early Imperial periods, legionary commanders were often the sons of senators who were using the army as a means of proving their mettle, gaining a reputation and so winning the political power that came with military glory by means of the well-trodden *cursus honorum*, the traditional 'career path' of the upper classes. To have a good military record was certainly to increase one's promotional prospects, though it goes without saying that, as always, money and the nepotism that comes from having influential family connections also talked. However, such cosy arrangements all changed by the fourth century as a result of the severance of all the old close ties back to Rome. In a macro-shift that few at the time could possibly have envisioned, the army stopped being a necessary, but perhaps unwelcome, interlude for well-bred young men who wanted to make it in Rome, and instead started to function as a lever of social mobility. The army in fact became an excellent career option, made attractive with some excellent prospects both for personal glory, power, influence and advancement (for those blessed with luck and ability, of course) for lower class men who under the old power structures would have lacked the money and family name that were really necessary to attain or successfully wield much actual power.

The local recruitment of troops was not only expedient for legions stationed on the frontier, it was vital to maintain the strength of the army. Recruitment from the traditional central provinces became increasingly difficult as military service became less and less attractive to those types and classes of men whom it had previously enticed. The emperor Severus had the foresight to understand something of the dynamic that was at play, and so he raised pay and improved conditions in an attempt to improve recruitment. His attempts were no doubt welcome to those men serving, but ultimately this move proved unsuccessful as recruitment from Italy itself hardly increased; presumably the trend towards Rome's demotion as a centre of power and the rise of the power of the outlying regions, was so well-entrenched by that time that these cosmetic changes did little to have any drastic effect.

To bridge the recruitment gap, emperors recruited increasing numbers of so-called 'barbarians'. For example, Illyria was a particularly popular recruiting ground, and recruits from that region fought fearlessly in defence of the empire against enemies both foreign and domestic. The name of Illyria went before them: Illyrians had long had a reputation for the quality of their fighting men, dating as far back as the period before Philip and Alexander the Great. (Alexander even had a contingent of several thousand Illyrians to accompany him on his war of conquest in Asia.)

In the early third century, these foreign recruits would have been thoroughly integrated into the legions and at least partially 'Romanised'. For example, they would have been trained in Roman battle tactics, used Roman equipment and been commanded by Romans. First and foremost in the process of Romanisation, they would have had to learn at least some Latin in order to get by, though it is a well-observed linguistic phenomenon that when two or more people of different native tongues are gathered together in a context in which common communication is necessary (and it is hard to imagine any other situation where common and easily understood discourse would have been of more importance than that of a battlefield), a lingua franca, known as a pidgin, emerges. This hybrid consists of a mixture of the features of the original languages.[1] (Thus, although the Roman army still 'officially' worked in the prestige language of Latin (the language in which written documents were still sent out from Rome and back again) there can be little doubt that the men on the ground, in managing their day-to-day life, communicated in an interesting Latin/'barbarian' pidgin.

But by the beginning of the fourth century, this situation was somewhat changed because there was not the exact same mixing up of men from many different places. Instead, Illyrians and others fought under their own national or tribal commanders; they used their own equipment and were not always integrated into the structure of a legion as a matter of course. Indeed, it could be argued that they were not, in fact, part of the Roman army at all, and certainly not in the way they had been, with the multiculturalism that used to obtain. Rather, they were essentially mercenaries who were being paid to fight for Rome, and this they did with vigour, but with much more of a sense of being separate and distinct.

A highly useful source to consider at this point is the Greek language *Strategikon*, purported to have been written by the emperor Maurice who reigned at the end of the sixth century. It is a work full of military detail covering many aspects of the craft of war, such as equipment, weaponry, armour, tactics, logistics, organisation, operation and the nature of the barbarian; so much so that it reads like a textbook or handbook on the art of war. What makes this source particularly invaluable, besides the interesting nature of the content, is the fact that it comes from an insider: it therefore combines the real military experience of its purported author with a book-based learning and insight into the issues as outlined above from other writers on these topics. This is important, because it seems that Maurice looked not just to the more literary works on war, but to the kinds of administrative documentation, official record keeping and other non-literary but nevertheless very important sources for his own account. This therefore gives his late sixth century account a relevance to the time we are dealing with; if Maurice has drawn directly on material such as that described, by creating a compilation of these kinds of sources, then he can be studied as an author who provides us with a direct link back to what would be an otherwise inaccessible fourth century world of war.

Thus, if we look at what Maurice has to say on the ethnic makeup of the army in his own time, it would seem that this so-called 'barbarizing' trend had progressed so far that steppe nomads had an influence on the shaping of Roman military equipment:

> They [soldiers] should have hooded coats of mail reaching to their ankles, which can be caught up by thongs and rings, along with carrying cases; helmets with small plumes on top; bows suited to the strength of each man, and not above it, more in fact on the weaker side, cases broad enough so that when necessary they can fit the strung bows in them, with spare bow strings in their saddle bags; quivers with covers holding about thirty or forty arrows; in their baldrics small files and awls; cavalry lances of that Avar type with leather thongs in the middle of the shaft and with pennons; swords, round neck pieces of the Avar type made with linen fringes and wool inside.[2]

In Constantine's time, these barbarian units had various loose designations, such as *foederati* or *auxilia* (both Latin names); *symmachoi* or *misthotoi* (both Greek in origin, both being a designation for 'mercenaries').[3] In particular, the *foederati* were a cavalry unit, and in Constantine's time had their own distinct sense of identity as a result of their targeted ethnic recruitment. They had also been permanently established, whereas in other cases, the barbarian units were of a more fluid and impermanent nature, created for individual operations and disbanded afterwards. These kind of one-off units operated autonomously but with Roman supplies, and they came from many places, in particular the Danube. For example, there were many Goths fighting under Licinius against Constantine in 324, and after this campaign these units would have been dispersed.

Although this situation had the advantage of enabling men of the same racial heritage to work and think as a group (surely easier to manage when they start with something as important as having a native language in common) it also had its own severe disadvantage. The strength that came from this kind of segregation was also a fatal flaw: it turned out to be dangerous in so far as it was the case that these troops had no historical, traditional loyalty to Rome, no sense of personal loyalty to their Roman commanders (because they were no longer commanded by Romans in the field, though they were supplied by them), no particular allegiance to what must have seemed to them a very abstract idea of empire, if indeed they had one at all, or to a remote emperor whose image they likely only ever saw on coins. The severance of the physical ties to Rome made real the severance of the conceptual: there was not the same sense of trust, co-operation, *esprit de corps*, loyalty or personal honour that there no doubt had been, and as a result, these troops could far more easily be paid off to change sides and support a usurper at a key moment. But what else to expect from mercenaries, who fight for the highest bidder? However, although these sections of the Roman army had some chance to go rogue, and despite some instances of disloyalty, this 'provincialised' army still fought well in defence of Rome, and the question of why this was so is something to explore further.

Perhaps one answer is that the Roman army, itself changing as its recruitment base changed, became the new locus of loyalty and honour, where once it may have been more for the glory and honour of Rome and the emperor. As has already been noted, the new pay structure, as well as the new command structure, made the army an appealing prospect for men from the lower social classes. Since there were fewer aristocratic men attracted to service in the army in the first place, senior ranks were no longer dominated by the sons of senators, and commanders were frequently promoted from within the ranks, rather than brought in from outside, which is an indication of an increased professionalism at work. These men who had worked their way up to higher and higher command had the distinct advantage of actually having established their own reputation and a personal relationship with their men, and of course they had experience of warfare from the front. Many senior commanders had had long and distinguished careers, which itself improved the operational effectiveness of the army. It was to be expected that commanders would know what they were doing. In comparison, during earlier periods a legion could be considered lucky indeed were it to be assigned an aristocratic commander who happened to understand the art of war.

This unwritten policy (of army as lever of social mobility) was essentially codified by Gallienus when he completely removed senators from the command of the army.[4] This ensured that men from the lowliest background could rise to a position of authority and power without also having to enter the political arena by becoming senators (which no doubt brought with it some grubby realpolitik), a role which many provincials, by virtue of lacking aristocratic manners and connections, were simply just not suited to. This stated change of policy made recruitment from the provinces even more attractive, and further reduced the numbers being recruited from Italy as opposed to elsewhere, thus accelerating the severing of the bond between the individual soldier and Rome. To summarise thus far: joining a legion that was stationed fairly locally to your own home became a better career choice for many men who were at the lower end of the social hierarchy and who had the skills, talents, abilities and ambitions desirable for war.

While we have historians such as Zosimus, Eusebius, the *Anonymus Valesianus*, Ammianus Marcellinus and the corpus of Latin Panegyrics to look to for accounts of battles, campaigns and sequences of events for this period, we are fortunate to have a rather unusual source on more general military matters in the form of Publius Flavius Vegetius Renatus and his *Epitoma Rei Militaris* (trans: Epitome of Military Science). Vegetius also wrote on veterinary medicine, but in this context his broad discussion of those military matters he considers in need of improvement (such as those of army recruitment and training; tactics and operations or naval warfare), which is thought to date from anywhere within 383–450 is useful indeed. Since Vegetius' aim is to write on those military matters which concern him, those which he considers to be a problem, it is notable that he selects the very issue of recruitment, and specifically barbarian recruitment as a key cause of what he sees as the on-going enervation of the Roman army.

For example, here Vegetius discusses the sources of the best soldiers and the principles of recruitment under the heading 'From what regions recruits should be levied':

> The order of our subject demands that the first part should treat of the provinces and peoples from which recruits should be levied. Now it is common knowledge that cowards and brave men are born in all places. However, nation surpasses nation in warfare, and climate exerts an enormous influence on the strength of minds and bodies. In this connection let us not omit what has won the approval of the most learned men. They tell us that all peoples that are near the sun, being parched by great heat, are more intelligent but have less blood, and therefore lack steadiness and confidence to

fight at close quarters, because those who are conscious of having less blood are afraid of wounds. On the other hand, the peoples of the north, remote from the sun's heat, are less intelligent, but having a superabundance of blood are readiest for wars. Recruits should therefore be raised from the more temperate climes. The plenteousness of their blood supplies a contempt for wounds and death, and intelligence cannot be lacking either which preserves discipline in camp and is of no little assistance with counsel in battle.[5]

Vegetius here recommends a different type of barbarian recruitment to that which he currently sees in operation. To continue, he next considers whether it is city or country dwellers which make the best soldiers:

The next question is to consider whether a recruit from the country or from the city is more useful. On this subject I think that it could never have been doubted that the rural populace is better suited for arms. They are nurtured under the open sky in a life of work, enduring the sun, careless of shade, unacquainted with bathhouses, ignorant of luxury, simple-souled, content with a little, with limbs toughened to endure every kind of toil, and for whom wielding iron, digging a fosse and carrying a burden is what they are used to from the country.[6]

Typically, Vegetius is keen to see a return to what he views as the golden age of the Roman army, and this includes the kind of recruitment model which he feels is currently out of favour but which served the empire well in its glory days of the first century. This suggests that Vegetius, from a civilian but educated position, sees the current socio-economic background of the army recruits as problematic, wishing instead for a different quality and calibre of man. Lastly, the great need for raw recruits in the army of the later Roman Empire probably meant that men from a wider age range were recruited. Vegetius disapproves:

At what age recruits should be approved: next let us examine at what age it is appropriate to levy soldiers. Indeed if ancient custom is to be retained, everyone knows that those entering puberty should be brought to the levy. For those things are taught not only more quickly but even more completely which are learned from boyhood. Secondly military alacrity, jumping and running should be attempted before the body stiffens with age. For it is speed which, with training, makes a brave warrior. Adolescents are the ones to recruit.[7]

All in all, Vegetius' *Epitoma* is interesting in that it tells us that a great many changes had taken place in the military and social fabric, such that an educated outsider (a man such as Vegetius), though knowledgeable and well-meaning, could wish for a return to the good old days (impossible though it was) based on an idealised first century AD Roman army, though of course those days and that reality had long gone.

Therefore, if it is true that the changing social and economic reality of the Roman Empire in the latter half of the third century and into Constantine's own reign served to shape and mould the army into a different kind of organisation, able to meet those needs, then it is also the case that the structural realities of the army in the years preceding Constantine's own reign, and the years of his reign, created new social realities of their own.

For example, the increasing number of military crises in the latter half of the third century and the fact that it was customary for the emperor to lead offensive expeditions meant that the emperor was more and more on campaign during this period rather than on other administrative or imperial duties. Inevitably, a closer link was therefore forged between emperor and army, by this very fact. There grew up a new and informal name for the troops who were led by the emperor: the mobile field army (in Latin: *comitatenses*). The centre of the *comitatenses* was the *legio II Parthica*, and radiating out from this core were detachments (in Latin: *vexillationes*) from legions, and completely new units, cavalry in particular. As mentioned, these had more of a distinct sense of themselves and had their own internal unity.

In conclusion, we can therefore state that the social dimension, the social context of the army, was much changed by Constantine's time and that these wider socio-economic factors themselves did much to shape and reform the Roman army.

Chapter 3

The Rise of Constantine:
Army, Tetrarchy and Frontiers

The Tetrarchy and the rise of Constantine

Tetrarchy is derived from the Greek, from *tessera* (four) and *archô* (rule) and thus means rule by four individuals. In writing the history of the Roman period, the term has taken on a specific connotation: it refers to the type of power structure formed at the end of the third-century crisis as a means of dividing up the overwhelming power which was held by a single emperor, and so making it possible that a number of military crises could be addressed simultaneously by professional commanders in the field.

For the origins of the formation of the Tetrarchy, we turn to Diocletian. Diocletian had no outstanding talent as a soldier, although with his military experience behind him to draw on, he was at least competent. It became quickly apparent to him that he did not have the military ability to control the entirety of the Roman Empire by himself. He also quickly realised that a new order had to be introduced, and that a means had to be found to increase the number of threats that could be countered simultaneously. His simple response was to introduce the first stages of the Tetrarchy, and this new power structure was first established in 285, though he then had to solve the problem of who to share power with. The solution was to raise Maximian to the rank of Caesar in that year and to give him command of the western provinces, an unprecedented move which was undoubted much to Maximian's surprise.

This worked as follows: Diocletian continued to rule in the eastern provinces, while Maximian was made co-emperor in the west. They each carried the title 'Augustus' (from the Latin *augustus*, plural *augusti*: venerable, majestic, august) in order to signify that they were co-emperors and that (in theory) neither was more senior than the other. Diocletian had quickly promoted Maximian in rank in order to free himself to deal with urgent issues on the Danube, while at the same time in effect creating an army under Maximian to deal with other issues in Gaul. There, the so-called *bacaudae* (miscellaneous wandering bands of discontented peasants, former soldiers and other types of disenfranchised people who hadn't got anything, and so hadn't got anything to lose), had risen up against Roman rule. Instability in Gaul also increased the likelihood of Franks and others from across the Rhine trying to capitalise on internal Roman weaknesses and difficulties. The two leaders of the *bacaudae*, Aelianus and Amandus, may have even proclaimed themselves emperors in a direct and provocative move intended to assert power on their own terms, rather than under those of the Romans.

Diocletian evidently realised the benefits of the policy of power sharing, and Maximian was quickly raised to the status of Augustus by his troops on 1 April 286. Diocletian apparently approved of this promotion, but was perhaps not in a position to oppose it even if he had wished. At first glance, Maximian seems like a rather curious choice for Diocletian to have promoted. The sources seem to present him as rather coarse and uncouth and possessing of quite a temper. The two had been friends of long-standing, however, and the fact that they were both from the same region (near Sirmium in modern Serbia) could also have played a part.

Maximian acted quickly in his new role and by the spring of 286 the revolt had been crushed after a series of minor engagements. For the following four or five years, Maximian fought almost constant battles against the Alamanni, the Burgundi and the Franks. Neither was Diocletian idle during this period, he too had difficulties with foreign invaders. He twice defeated the Sarmatae (289 and 293) in the region of the Danube; defeated the Persian Sassanids in Syria (299) and suppressed a native revolt in Egypt (291).[1]

It will be noted by the attentive reader that so far, we have only considered two, not four men, in a power-sharing system.[2] For many years this power system of two-man rule, or Diarchy, had worked successfully, in much the same way as Agrippa had acted as a foil to Augustus in the early imperial period (although Agrippa was more obviously Augustus' junior partner, and so it was well understood that there was a clear hierarchy in operation). Both Diocletian and Maximian evidently realised that the enormity of the task of ruling and defending the Roman Empire was such that, even when divided between two men, each still required a deputy. Diocletian therefore decided to move one step further: in 293 he determined to make a further structural change to effect a full Tetrarchy by promoting two other individuals to the status of Caesar (the title Maximian had initially held). Each of the two Augusti was to appoint a junior colleague who would carry the title Caesar, intended to indicate that they were only subordinate to the Augusti themselves. These two men – Caesars – were Galerius and Constantius Chlorus.

In the context of both internal and external instability, it was believed that four powerful men were required partly because the Roman Empire was beset from almost every side by foreign aggressors, and partly because (as already noted) the size and complexity of the Roman Empire made the task of dealing with these threats too massive for one man alone. In order to combat these numerous problems, the four rulers stationed themselves throughout the Empire and each commanded a mobile field army. The reality of having a power structure based around four, rather than one, man in charge did of course necessitate that each man had his own *comitatenses*, and these *comitatenses* were themselves jigsaw-like; they were made up of distinct detachments and units taken from elsewhere; a bricolage but one wherein each jigsaw piece was its own functioning, discrete whole that did not necessarily need to have all that much to do with another, beyond slotting alongside it in battle. For example, Diocletian's own *comitatenses* was made up from the legions of the *Ioviani* and *Herculiani* alongside some elite cavalry and subdivisions of other units.

Diocletian, as the eastern Augustus, made his capital and base of operations at Nicomedia in Asia Minor (modern Izmit, in Turkey). From here he could get into the Balkans with speed, whilst also being able to defend the eastern borders from Persian (Sassanid) invasion. Maximian, as the western Augustus, stationed himself in Mediolanum (Milan) from which he had the ability to defend Gaul and northern Italy, as well as North Africa, after only a short naval trip.

Of the two Caesars, Galerius, the eastern Caesar, made Sirmium (Sremska Mitrovica in Serbia) his base of operations. This had obvious strategic importance as a base to defend from invasion from across the Danube. Constantius Chlorus, the western of the two Caesars, made his capital Augusta Treverorum (Trier in Germany). This region was, again, strategically vital in offering protection for the Empire from invasion by barbarians across the Rhine. Although they had fixed capitals to act as their bases of operation, they also had the possibility of being able to respond to threats from outside their immediate locale.

In 296, the eastern Empire was threatened by a new and ambitious Persian king: Narses. Mesopotamia had been ceded to the previous Persian king, Bahram in 284, but his successor was not content with this throw of the dice. Diocletian assigned Galerius, his Caesar in the east, to deal with the invasion, and after an initial defeat at Carrhae, Galerius retreated to Armenia and crushed the Persian army there in a second battle, quickly following this up with the capture of Ctesiphon. However, from the platform of this success further gains into the east were not developed. Instead, this victory was used for the re-establishment of the frontier.

Each of these four senior generals commanded a mobile field army, as already discussed. This conferred the advantage of a tremendous flexibility to deal with threats on a number of fronts simultaneously. For example, in 298 Constantius was engaged on the Rhine frontier against the Franks, whilst Maximian was fighting in North Africa.[3] In the earlier history of the Roman Empire, whenever two powerful men commanded an army there was generally a civil war. With four powerful men, each commanding their own forces, one might imagine that civil war would be the immediate result, but initially at least it was not. This is probably because of the number of foreign enemies that were harassing the empire; this meant that the attentions of the Augusti and Caesars were fully engaged in dealing with the external enemies so that there was little time left for worrying about internal rivalries.

In late 303, Diocletian visited Rome to celebrate his twenty years of rule. The years of constant campaigning were evidently beginning to take their toll on the ageing Augustus, and early in 304 he apparently made the decision that both he and Maximian should retire and abdicate their positions of authority when the latter had also celebrated his twentieth year in power. This suggestion initially met with a negative response from his colleague, Maximian, but eventually Maximian was persuaded. On 1 May 305 both emperors abdicated their positions, after first swearing an oath in the Temple of Jupiter to retire completely from public life. Diocletian retired to Nicomedia and Maximian to Milan.

When Diocletian and Maximian jointly abdicated, this left a huge power vacuum at the top of the Roman state. However this was filled when the two Caesars, Constantius Chlorus and Galerius, were simultaneously promoted to the rank of Augustus to replace Diocletian and Maximian. Naturally, this left two vacancies in the Tetrarchy for Caesars, which were considerably less easy to fill. The tried-and-tested dynastic principle suggested that the two Caesars should be Maxentius, the son of Maximian and Constantine, son of Constantius. In line with the innovation of the Tetrarchy concept, Diocletian, however, flew in the face of Roman tradition and thought that heredity was not a solid foundation on which to build the rule of the Roman Empire. It appears he felt that Maxentius was not up to the job of Caesar, and so, rather than resort to the claims of heredity in one case but not the other, he ignored the claims of both these men and instead appointed Severus II (western Caesar) a friend of Galerius, and Maximinus II Daia (eastern Caesar), the nephew of Galerius.

The Roman Empire was again divided between four men in a Tetrarchy. Constantius held Britain, Gaul and Spain whilst his Caesar, Severus, held

Africa, Italy and Pannonia. Galerius controlled Asia Minor and his Caesar, Maximianus held the remainder of the Asiatic provinces as well as Egypt.[4] Constantius was theoretically the senior of the two Augusti, as Diocletian had been before him, but in reality he was in a weak position strategically. Galerius controlled the east and through his friendship with Severus, could practically exert considerable authority in the west as well. Of the two, Galerius had undoubtedly got the better of the deal.

In 305/6, Britain again was under threat from the Picts in the north of the country. Constantius was forced to return to Britain, having already spent a considerable length of time stationed there. In this campaign, Constantius saw his opportunity to aid the promotion of his son, Constantine. He made a request of Galerius to allow him to be joined on the campaign by his son; Galerius, fearing ultimately the potential for civil war if he refused, could do little but acquiesce. Constantine had been in Rome at the time, but he made a dash to join his father at Boulogne just prior to their journey into Britain.

Constantius and Constantine conducted a campaign in Britain which reached as far as the north of Scotland in early 306, successfully suppressing the potential uprising. Once the campaign was completed, both men withdrew to Eboracum (York), where Constantius died. This set the scene for a new and interesting twist of fate: before any of the remaining three senior commanders could act, Constantius' old legions proclaimed Constantine to be the new Augustus. Constantine was not naive in matters of power, and he could see that this put him in a somewhat awkward position in relation to the rest of the Tetrarchy. Thus, he did not assume that this affirmation from the ranks automatically translated into real power. Rather, he sent a communication to Galerius informing him of what had occurred and no doubt declaring his position that he should legitimately be considered Augustus in replacement of his father.

However, neither was Constantine a man to look a gift horse in the mouth. In order to try and capitalise on the backing he had of his men, Constantine quickly moved into southern Gaul. Here he received a communication from Galerius offering a compromise solution, whereby Severus was to be declared the new Augustus while Constantine took the title of Caesar, again strengthening further the position of Galerius. The net effect of this promotion was to leave Maximian's son, Maxentius, who had not been incorporated into the Tetrarchy, as far away from a position of real power as ever, and this goaded him into action. Maxentius took matters into his own hands and, in October 306, carried out a coup in Rome and seized power. The basis of his coup was over taxation, always a common and popular bone of contention with the Roman citizenry. Africa and southern Italy went over to Maxentius, whereas northern Italy remained loyal to Severus.

Maxentius realised that strategically he was in a weak position; he commanded the Praetorian Guard and a few urban cohorts from Rome, but little else, and certainly not enough of an army to resist the *comitatenses* of any one of the Tetrarchy. Therefore, with the approval of the senate (though were they really in a position to refuse?), he sent a request to his recently-retired father asking that he return to public office and resume his previous position. Despite this meaning that he would break an oath sworn in the Temple of Jupiter a little over a year previously, Maximian did indeed come out of retirement and he resumed the rank of Augustus in February 307. Maximian took the further step of issuing coins praying for a thirty year rule, having previously retired after twenty years as Augustus alongside Diocletian.[5]

Despite his retirement and period of absence from the political life of the Empire, Maximian still commanded considerable respect, authority and influence over his contemporaries. He persuaded or otherwise prevented, first Severus and later Galerius from invading Italy, thus protecting his son's fledgling position in Rome (and naturally, his own as well). Nevertheless, there was weakness in this arrangement: both Maxentius and Maximian realised that at some point Galerius would have to move against them, and they were simply not militarily strong enough to resist. An alliance with Constantine, who was now positioned in Gaul, seemed the obvious solution, so Maximian moved into Gaul, where he engineered a very useful marriage alliance by sealing the engagement of Constantine to his daughter Fausta (Maxentius' sister). Maxentius was correct to expect Galerius to act, and he did not have to wait long. Galerius entered Italy but did not have the siege train strong enough to attack the capital, so he withdrew his forces. Perhaps because he was too well aware of his lack of military strength, Maxentius took no action against him at all, simply allowing him to withdraw unharried.

For reasons that remain unclear, Maximian, now re-established on the Roman stage, turned on his son. Maximian attempted to persuade Constantine to join him in attacking the retreating Galerius, and once he was removed from power, to continue on to Rome and remove Maxentius, Maximian's upstart son. Maximian no doubt tried to buy Constantine's support with the promise of him replacing Galerius as Augustus. But Constantine was not swayed, and once Spain declared support for the latter, he did no more power wrangling than to break off relations with Maximian.

Maximian went to Gaul to try and bring about an alliance for Maxentius with Constantine against Galerius. In order to sweeten the deal, Maximian gave Constantine the title Augustus and offered the hand of his daughter Fausta in marriage, as mentioned. However, in 308, Maximian had had a falling out with his son, for reasons that remain unclear, and he turned on him despite his recent return to the Roman state. But Maximian failed to depose him, so he sought out Constantine for support and shelter. After this, Maximian was still unable to leave politics alone, and after the conference of Carnuntum in late 308 he was again forced to retire; instead, he revolted against Constantine who had provided him with a haven from his son after their quarrel. This was his last mistake; he was captured at Massilia and committed suicide rather than capitulate as a means of regaining some honour at least in death.

Galerius, realising that the Tetrarchy was at risk of breaking down completely, attempted to persuade Diocletian to come out of retirement and attend a conference with the intention of resolving the current impasse. Diocletian refused, but did manage to persuade his one-time fellow Augustus, Maximian, to retire once more. In order to fill the position vacant after Maximian again stepped down, Licinianus Licinius was promoted to the rank of Augustus. After some considerable power brokering, all four men of the Tetrarchy: Galerius, Licinius, Constantine and Maximianus were all declared joint Augusti. Maxentius was declared a usurper despite still holding Italy, Spain and Africa.[6] Constantine had, therefore, managed to achieve for himself the rank of Augustus without the need for civil war to be declared, but that situation was not to last for long because as an ambitious man he was not content sharing power. His further rise to pre-eminence will be discussed later.

The Army: *comitatenses*

When Constantine was declared Emperor by his troops at Eboracum (York) in 306, he became one of four tetrarchs and joined Diocletian, Maximian and Galerius in power-sharing, essentially controlling one quarter of the Roman Empire. At his accession he inherited the army that had been commanded by his father, Constantius. In terms of organisation and quality there would have been little to decide between the armies commanded by each one of the tetrarchs, though each man would have naturally tried to make improvements that were advantageous to himself. For example, they would have attempted to improve the quality of their recruits and would have chosen to establish their own men in positions of authority in the legions in order to try and ensure loyalty.

To provide some context for understanding the army, we must return to the recent past: in 285, the armies commanded by the tetrarchs were quite small, as was necessary to maintain mobility. As mentioned, Diocletian's force comprised the legion of the *Ioviani* and the cavalry units, the *lanciarii* and the *comites*. Galerius on the other hand commanded three Moesian legions and the *equites promoti* cavalry regiment.[7] These core units would have been supplemented by others as and when they were necessary. There was nothing unusual about this arrangement; this had always been the case with Roman armies from the Republican period and beyond, though as noted there was more of a sense of these kinds of units having their own separate autonomy.

The mobile field armies that were ubiquitous during the later Roman period grew out of the turmoil of the third-century crisis and of the need to respond rapidly to the growing threats to the Roman Empire, but we must consider the question of who created them: Diocletian or Constantine? We know from the surviving source material that Diocletian had with him a *comitatus* (from the verb *comitari*, trans: accompany, follow, attend, and so literally means companion force of some kind) but this could simply refer to a group of commanders or advisors rather than a mobile field army per se; we do not know if any of the other tetrarchs were also accompanied by a *comitatus*. It could be that the *comitatus*, whatever they were, were the forerunner of the *comitatenses*, though this remains unclear. It seems likely that the initial idea was Diocletian's, coming out of the changing nature of military reality in the latter half of the third century, but was likely developed and extended by Constantine to become the much more powerful mobile field armies of the fourth century, around about after the Battle of the Milvian Bridge. What was made evident after this victory was that the forces Constantine had been accustomed to command would not suffice to control the empire. The improved *comitatenses* were the result; a more solid distinction was now made between the *comitatenses* and *limitanei*.[8] In short, Constantine probably completed a series of military reforms that had been initiated by Diocletian, but were grounded in the military reality of the Roman Empire of the time, though for administrative purposes the difference between *limitanei* and *comitatenses* was in length of service required, tax benefits due on retirement and the physical standards required for entry.

To look at the surviving textual evidence for this, the only direct evidence we have for the creation of the *comitatenses* comes from Constantine's reign itself. For example, there is a letter written by Constantine to Maximus in 325 which is recorded within the Theodosian Code, a fifth century record of Roman legislation, Book 7 of which is on military matters where they relate to the law:

> *Comitatenses, ripenses milites*, and *protectores* shall be exempt from the capitation tax on their own persons, as well as those of their fathers, mothers, and wives, if they survive, and if they have been enrolled as *capiti*. But if they should not have one of these, or if

they should have none of them, they will exempt, as their own *peculium*, only so much as they would have been able to exempt from these people if they had existed, and they shall not form agreements with other persons whereby they exempt the property of others by fraudulent ownership, but (they will only exempt) what they have.[9]

This section of Constantine's letter shows that there is a distinction between *comitatenses* and *ripenses* (since they are named as such) as well as the existence of another army grouping: the *protectores*, who were often men of long service. By the time of the fourth century, this rank had the function of staff officer, and the *protectores* were given the full title of *protectores domestici* to distinguish them from the *protectores* under the command of a *magister militum*. The *protectores domestici*, formed into *scholae* of *domestici peditum* and *domestici equitum* show up in the *Notitia Dignitatum*; the prestigious responsibility for being the personal guard of the emperor himself was accorded to men drawn from the *scholae* of *protectores domestici* who upon selection for this role took the title *candidati*.[10]

This section is from a text which as a whole is a letter addressed to a *vicarius*, an official who needs to know how to treat the men who had previously served under Licinius, thus indicating that the categories Constantine refers to here predate his own reign, and have their origins in an earlier time (though exactly when it is harder to say). To compare, in another section that follows on shortly from the one above, we see there being made the distinction between *comitatenses* and *ripenses* in terms of benefits due. For example:

If a soldier at any time or in any place has deserved a discharge, if he was discharged from the *comitatenses* by reason of age or disability, even though he had not served the requisite number of years, he will still have the exemption for himself and his wife. Soldiers discharged from the *ripenses*, will have the same privilege without discrimination, if they prove that they were discharged because of wounds they have suffered; if a person will leave military service after fifteen years but before twenty-four years, he will benefit only from the exemption of his own person; he will receive the benefit of the exemption for his wife as well if, as a *ripensis*, he leaves military service after twenty-four years.[11]

It is clear from this, that the category a soldier belongs to (whether *ripenses* or *comitatenses*) matters enough to be included in this discussion of discharge of the army and the benefits to be received from this. This indicates that by this time the distinction between the two had certainly been made, although again the roots of this division in the army certainly lie before Constantine's own time.

As noted, the *comitatenses* consisted of both infantry and elite cavalry units, as did the *limitanei*. The cavalry units were divided into *vexillationes* of 500 strong, and commanded by tribunes. The size of a Roman legion seems to have varied slightly throughout Roman history, but by the late third and early fourth century they were around 5,000 strong, divided between 10 cohorts. The *comitatenses* were commanded by a new rank in the army: the *magistri peditum* for the infantry and the *magistri equitum* for the cavalry, another change from direct command by the emperor (though at the beginning of Constantine's own reign he led the new field army himself).

Typically, the *comitatenses* were stationed at a strategically important city some distance from the frontier, but at a location that had good road links that would allow for a rapid deployment when necessary. Constantine was heavily criticised during the later Roman period, probably with some justification, for what was perceived as a policy of strengthening the mobile field armies at the expense of the frontier troops. This seems to have been especially true of the cavalry, but it affected the infantry too.[12] The size of the *comitatenses* suggests that they could not all have been stationed with Constantine and that they must have been spread throughout the Empire, as the armies of the tetrarchs had been only a few years previous. The commanders of these separate armies appear to have been relatively junior, and they certainly did not rival Constantine in authority or influence.

The Army: *limitanei*

The *limitanei* were the guardians of the borders of the Roman Empire. Since the reign of Hadrian, limits to the expansion of the empire had been considered, and once the empire had essentially stopped its steady outward march, there were borders that needed to be defended. Barbarians from outside of the empire were an increasing threat, and it was no longer considered acceptable to permit an invasion to happen while the emperor in Rome gathered troops and moved to meet it. In this era, the threats were far more frequent and widespread for this model to continue to work without risking serious instability. To go along with the mobile field armies, therefore, the border troops were a necessity.

The *limitanei* were either stationed in one of a series of border forts that were constructed all throughout the borders of the empire (the most famous being the *limes* in Germany) or they could equally be stationed on the Roman side of strategic rivers or roads where forts had not yet been constructed. Of the troops that constituted the *limitanei*, the auxiliary troops, along with the cavalry, were stationed directly on the frontier at key points, for example on Hadrian's Wall, or on the Rhine or Danube Rivers. The legionary troops were positioned at a distance from the frontier to allow some flexibility and speed of response if a nearby fort or position was under attack.

Unlike the *comitatenses*, who were now commanded by the two ranks of *magistri* (though they had been commanded by the emperor himself), the *limitanei* were commanded by *duces*, with the headquarters being under a *praefectus*. These *duces* (Latin singular: *dux*, leader or general; *duces* in the plural) were of more junior rank than the *magistri*, and the *limitanei* were paid at a lower rate, and had different benefits and so on due to them as mentioned, compared to the *comitatenses*. This stratification led to the allegation of a two-tier army, with the *limitanei* being considered second-class soldiers.

The history of the rank of *dux* also has its roots in the military turmoil of the second half of the third century; as the title of a rank, it came out of border regions where conflict was becoming more common. The power of a *dux* included the ability to command frontier regions, such as the *dux ripae Mesopotamiae* (trans: the leader/commander of the riverbank of Mesopotamia, in Dura-Europus) and also had the power to command small field armies. It was the sphere of influence and range of the *duces* that was expanded by Diocletian, who both made more of a separation between military and non-military service, in that a *dux* became more of specifically military, rather than civil or bureaucratic, role and he allowed a *dux* quite a wide range of command in terms of provinces covered. However, this structural change percolated through the system fairly slowly, and by Constantine's time there was still some cross-over between ranks which had both a military and non-military remit, although the aim of the creation and definition of the rank of *dux* was, of course, to make more of a definite separation between these two worlds.

Thinking back to the *limitanei/comitatenses* split, we do know that Diocletian was praised by Zosimus for repairing the many forts that already existed along the frontier. He also praised the emperor for redeploying troops into these forts.[13] In contrast, in the east of the empire, legions had been stationed in cities some distance from the frontier for many years, and this would not have seemed like any kind of innovation there, one indication of a parting of the ways between eastern and western empire.

While it is true to say that we do not know exactly when this military change of emphasis occurred, we do know that it was in place by 325 at the latest. A law of that date distinguishes between three types of troops: the *comitatenses*, the *ripenses* and the *alares/cohortales*. The implication of this law was that the *ripenses* were of a lesser status than the *comitatenses*, much as the *limitanei* were. It is perhaps the case that the term *limitanei* was not yet in common use, and became a fixed term only at a later time, and that the actual frontier troops were in position and called by another name. By the sixth century, the split between mobile field army and frontier troops was absolute; the latter being permanently stationed at their forts and acting as farmers of the local land as well as defenders of the frontier. During the fourth century, this division existed but was not quite as stark; as noted earlier, the best of the *limitanei* could, and frequently were, seconded permanently into the *comitatenses*.[14] Therefore, a two-tier army was certainly starting to evolve during the reign of Constantine, though this innovation had its roots in an earlier time.

Finally, we can briefly turn to the navy: at this time, the function of the navy was to support the land troops, and it was not considered a separate and distinct service in its own right. Fleets could be found in different locations throughout the empire, and these were used both for fighting and for equipping land troops and the transport of the same. Since Constantinople had such favourable geography, it became the prime fleet station in the east, and whenever naval engagements or strategies were necessary, they were under the command of army generals, thus indicating the secondary or subordinate nature of the Roman naval force as compared to the terrestrial.

The Army: Numbers

The organisation of the legions during the Republican and early imperial periods is fairly well established, but this is not the case for the later Roman Empire. The legions had always been subdivided into units that built up to the whole legion, and this appears to have remained the case. Some of these individual units could, and occasionally were, moved from one assignment to another or from one legion to another. Generally the transfer would come from the frontier army to the mobile field army.

During the third century and earlier, a legion consisted of around 5,000 men in 10 cohorts. This approximate figure continued after the third-century crisis and can be evidenced by the *Ioviani* and *Herculiani* legions. These were two newly recruited elite legions which were raised by Diocletian and Maximian and each were 6,000 men strong.[15] However, it is a truth universally acknowledged throughout the entire annals of military history that the paper strength of a unit is seldom its operational strength. Inevitable losses would have been sustained through continuous warfare, retirement and sickness (which were probably far worse than we appreciate, as suggested by the Vindolanda tablets). Some of the 'legions' were in fact very small, nothing more than *vexillationes*, similar to earlier periods, and commanded by a tribune: a more junior position than we would expect the commander of a full legion to be.

During the fourth century there developed a separation in the organisation of western and eastern legions. The eastern legions saw the development of *lanciarii*, or elite infantry, and of stronger cavalry units called *promoti*.[16] We know that in 299 *legio II Traiana* was stationed in Egypt and consisted of a *vexillatio* at Apollinopolis Superior, some *lanciarii* stationed at Ptolemais and some *promoti* at Tentyra. By the middle of the century many of these individual detachments had essentially become distinct bodies in their own right, and operated independently of what was the parent legion. Many of the legions in the *comitatus* were reduced in size to around 1,000 men due to this process, and were commanded by tribunes. This was not a quick or sudden process, but one of gradual change throughout the later third and early-fourth century.

How we can know this is partly thanks to an important primary source which increases our knowledge of the extent and structuring of the Roman army: the *Notitia Dignitatum* gives lists of military officials and their under-lings circa 400, allowing us to piece together some of the skeleton command structure of the army, on which we can flesh out more of the details of operation and function using other historians and source evidence.[17]

This occasional division of the traditional legions into smaller entities with more elite units gave far greater operational flexibility to the com-mander. Therefore, he could respond far more rapidly to invasions or uprisings than was possible during earlier periods. It became apparent that the changes in the eastern mobile field army needed to be mirrored in some way in the west. The western solution was rather different, however; instead of breaking down some of the legions into smaller more flexible units, an entirely new elite infantry force was created. These were called the *auxilia palatina* and were made up of non–citizens. Some of these new units would have been existing units detached from larger forces, but some were raised from scratch where they were needed. They were typically raised on the frontier regions because these were rich recruiting grounds for fresh blood in a way that Italy no longer was. These units were small, on the eastern model, and therefore also designed to be flexible and able to respond speedily to invasions, uprisings or general unrest.

In terms of the total size of the forces the emperor commanded in the fourth century, it is almost exclusively considered the case by historians that the fourth century army was considerably larger than that of the first century. However, to make any sort of estimate, we must engage in a certain amount of speculation. Agathias in the sixth century gives a total for the entirety of the Roman army at 645,000. He noted that this was: 'in the old days' which is usually believed to be during the reign of Constantine, or at least around that time. John Lydus, another sixth century writer and imperial secretary, gave the suspiciously accurate figure of 389,704 men in the army and 45,562 in the navy for Diocletian's forces. His position in the empire suggests that he may well have had access to official (presumed accurate) records and archives, and thus the number may actually be a good estimation rather than a suspicious plucking of a figure out of the air. If we do assume that Lydus' figure for the Roman navy was close to accurate, then Agathias' total for the land based army would have been around 600,000.[18] This would have required at least 15,000 new recruits every year, and perhaps as many as double that.

In all likelihood, however, this figure of 600,000 represented the on-paper strength for the army but, as noted earlier, armies in the Roman world would very seldom have been at their paper strength, especially during a period of sustained conflict. We have no real idea how large the shortfall would be through sickness and combat losses, but a third seems plausible. This would mean an actual strength of around 400,000, close to Lydus' figure, but with the provisos as noted, this is speculation based on the data available, such as it is.

To put this into context: the first century army commanded by Tiberius was around 255,000 men, as implied by the incisive work of Tacitus.[19] This increase in the size of the army came largely from men on the fringes of the empire and from those whom educated Romans would have dismissed as being 'barbarians'. As noted, this state of affairs is indicative of the far greater difficulties that the later Roman Empire was faced with as compared to the post-Augustan period, and also that by Constantine's time the army was no longer a single uniform body, but had rather evolved into a complex and multifaceted beast which exhibited a high degree of regional variation.

To make another brief mention of naval numbers: in 324, Constantine's fleet totalled around 200 warships at least and 2,000 plus transports. In comparison, Licinius held 350 warships, though it is hard to determine the exact size and reach of the navy since it was a common practice to requisition merchant ships for military use as and when required (for example, for a civil war) meaning that the reality of the size and power of the navy during an engagement or operation could actually be much larger than these figures would suggest.

The Army: Command Structure

Before the third-century crisis, the organisation of the command structure of the army was relatively easy to discern. The military might of the empire was divided between the legions, which were stationed in potentially trouble-some or volatile provinces like Britain, Syria and on the great frontier rivers of the Rhine and Danube. Each of these legions was controlled by the provincial governor in whose province they were stationed, and of course ultimately, they were at the beck-and-call of the emperor if he so desired. As already discussed, however, by the fourth century these large and relatively cumbersome legions were no longer fit for the purpose of defending the empire against the different and increasing threats with which it was faced. Many of these large legions were also broken up, with sections being moved to the frontiers permanently and other units becoming the core of the *comitatenses*.

It is likely that Diocletian not only began the process of breaking up the legions, which Constantine continued to its completion, but he also broke up the old civil command structure. Instead of a local governor controlling the legion (often a man with little or no military experience) the military duties were assigned to a man in a newly created position: *dux*, a rank already discussed. The civil running of the province was left in the hands of the provincial governor. This system is close to that employed by Alexander the Great in his newly conquered provinces, where typically the civil government was left in the hands of a local governor and the military was commanded by a native Macedonian. For Alexander, this arrangement was about trust and security; for Diocletian and Constantine it was about operational flexibility and effectiveness. In each case, the means was much the same.

The solution of Diocletian meant that these *duces* could operate between provinces and were not tied down to a particular area any longer; having said this, however, in practice there was a rough general area in which they would operate most of the time. For example, there were two *ducates* in Britain, twelve on the Rhine and Danube frontier and eight in the eastern provinces with a further seven in Africa.[20]

As with most of the military reforms at the end of the third century and into the fourth, this was a gradual process, and there is no single date that we can ascribe to their introduction. That the *dux* would have a purely military role was also not entirely clear from the outset. During the early fourth century, the *duces* occasionally undertook roles that later would become the purview of the provincial governor, though as already discussed, it seems to have been Diocletian's aim to draw more of a line between the military and civilian in the rank of the *dux*, although this evidently did not become the reality for all *duces* who were perhaps still working on more than one front even in Constantine's own time.

The separation of military and civil function in the provinces had profound effects upon the empire and its citizens, and it is likely that these were not completely intended, or indeed, foreseen. With the military role of the *dux* now made separate from the civil role of the provincial governor, the upshot of this change was that military leaders could be chosen on merit for the first time. The quality of men being chosen for military roles would have improved as a result. From the fourth century onwards it was no longer the case that senior military figures were in their positions because they were the sons of wealthy senators who were using the army as a stop–gap means of establishing or improving on their reputations before returning to Rome to take up a comfortable political career. This type of individual had been a blight on the professionalism of the legions since the Republican period, and now the far-reaching military restructuring and changing nature of warfare in the later Roman Empire sounded its death knell.

Instead, wealthy and aristocratic young men who wished to pursue a senatorial career still had the opportunities to do so, by first operating as provincial governors (and their opportunities were not restricted in this regard), but they would no longer be able to claim military success. This would not have been any kind of a significant drawback for them (and was possibly welcomed, since military service was never exactly renowned for its ease or comfort), because the same would have been true of all of their contemporaries in the senate.

For dedicated military men, however, the change was profound. Ambitious and competent soldiers could now have a long and successful career in the army without a glass ceiling based on class snobbery to hold them back. They could quite literally start at the bottom and ultimately attain the rank of *dux* (always assuming they had the right qualities and a certain amount of luck). This was especially the case for men born outside of the historically-favoured recruiting grounds of Italy. Increasingly, soldiers were recruited from frontier zones where there was a seemingly endless supply of willing and very capable soldiers, all of whom were prepared to fight in the name of Rome and in the name of their own personal advancement. With recruiting happening almost exclusively in these frontier zones, the natural outcome was that the men who were being promoted through the ranks were also from these areas. And so very soon, the army was composed and commanded almost entirely by men from outside Italy: a significant demographic shift in the make-up of the military had thus taken place.

Once Constantine had defeated his final internal rival (Licinius) to become the sole ruler of the Empire, the military reforms continued and could now be enacted upon the entirety of the armed forces. The *duces* continued to command the *limitanei*, but two new offices were created within the field army, with a different remit: *magister peditum* and *magister equitum* (master of the infantry and cavalry respectively):

> After thus dividing the office of the prefects, he was anxious to reduce their influence still further; for whereas the commanders of the soldiers everywhere used to be centurions and tribunes and *duces* who held the rank of generals in each place, Constantine set up *magistri militum*, one of horse, the other of infantry, and to these he transferred power to command the troops and to punish those guilty of crimes, depriving the prefects of this authority.[21]

However, the distinction in rank was not as stark and clear-cut as the two titles may lead us to think. Both can be found commanding each section of the field army, and collectively they were called *magistri militum*: 'masters of soldiers'. These two offices were a change from the early Empire, however, when the infantry were unquestionably the elite units, and cavalry were little more than scouts and messengers. From the creation of the *comitatenses*, their status was much closer to being equal, although the infantry probably remained of a slightly higher status overall. The requirement for mobility and flexibility had been fundamental in forcing the change, as had the move away from recruiting primarily Italian troops for the legions towards recruiting from some regions where cavalry were historically stronger than infantry.

The *magistri militum* were of a more senior position within the military hierarchy than the *duces*, and this would have contributed to an increased separation between the frontier troops and the field army. However, there would never have been any doubt over which was of the higher status within the Empire.[22] Nevertheless, whether *dux* or *magister militum*, having a position of operational command in the Roman army did still require a similar skill set. This necessity is made clear by Vegetius, who describes the kind of intelligence and preparation required to perform the role of *dux* or *magister militum* well:

> [A good general] should have itineraries of all regions in which war is being waged written out in the fullest detail, so that he may learn the distances between places by the number of miles and the quality of roads, and examine short-cuts, by-ways, mountains and rivers accurately described. Indeed the more conscientious generals reportedly had itineraries of the provinces in which the emergency occurred not just annotated but illustrated as well, so that they could choose their route when setting out by the visual aspect as well as by mental calculation.[23]

After the death of Constantine, the *comitatus* was broken up into three separate armies: one in the east, one in Illyricum and one in Gaul, each commanded by one of Constantine's sons. There was evidently considerable cooperation between the armies, and the transferral of troops was a relatively common occurrence. By the end of the reign of Constantine, the net outcome was that the Roman army was probably more flexible and able to perform its core function than at any time since the early empire.

The Army: Equipment

As was necessary to sustain military operations, Roman military equipment continued to be manufactured in great quantities during the fourth century. Surprisingly, and despite almost all of the recruitment now coming from the border regions, the army continued to be trained and equipped mostly along the old and traditional Roman legionary lines. The Roman army of the reign of Constantine would, therefore, have looked much the same as its earlier imperial counterpart, in so far as the infantry of the *comitatenses* would have carried a sword, spear and shield and been equipped with a cuirass and helmet.[24]

However, there were some small changes to the equipment of the army. The third century saw the development of cataphracts (in Latin: *clibanarii*) within the Roman order of battle. These were heavily armoured cavalry units and were not new in the annals of warfare, but they were new to Rome. They had been employed by Darius against Alexander the Great, and were ubiquitous in Hellenistic armies, but Romans had never shown much of a willingness to develop their always-limited cavalry in this direction before the third century.

Roman infantry began to use the longer two–edged cavalry sword, called the *spatha* (around 0.7 to 0.9 m long) as a replacement to the traditional and shorter *gladius*. One drawback was that the *spatha* was too long to use effectively when in a tight formation, but the infantry did not always fight in this way, so it was more useful during some types of encounters rather than others. Also, the infantry made use of other secondary weapons such as axes and maces. The infantry also carried with them a short sword that would be more effective for close order fighting, as it was intended. This was known as a *semispatha* by Vegetius. The *pilum* of earlier centuries was also replaced by a much heavier spear. The *pilum* was often used as a missile weapon, whereas the new spear, the *hasta*, was too heavy for this. As well as the *hasta*, a soldier could also carry a throwing spear, which was slightly longer than the earlier and lighter *pilum* (which is in fact usually translated as 'javelin') thus show-ing that there were a variety of throwing weapons which had a short range available. A further fourth century innovation that greatly increased the fire power of the Roman army was the *plumbata*, and these were essentially short and light weighted darts. Each trooper would carry up to six of these, and they could be thrown at short range into the enemy formations. This would have the same impact as several volleys of arrows, but their advantage was that they could be better directed. Therefore, the front lines of the enemy could be decimated as battle was about to be joined; the key moment when the cohesion of a tightly packed infantry body was most vital. Finally, infantry and cavalry archers carried different bows, as would be expected: infantry bows were larger than the cavalry, these last being more compact to make them fit for purpose for horseback deployment.

Roman choices for hand-to-hand fighting weapons did therefore change. The traditional close quarters combat involving the *gladius* as the primary weapon was now replaced with the more traditionally Greek style of using spears as the primary offensive weapon. This should not be seen as a retrograde step, but rather as a defensive one: it was a means of providing greater protection to the troops as the enemy had to fight their way through many spear tips before they could even start to engage the legionary troopers.[25] We should also note that in comparison, the offensive capability of a fourth century legion was far greater than its first century counterpart.

In terms of defensive equipment, legionaries of the early empire would most often wear the *lorica segmentata*, which was essentially segmented plate armour. This provided far greater defensive capability than either the chain mail or scale mail that Romans were also technologically capable of producing. However, there were several drawbacks: it was difficult to manufacture and maintain; expensive and resource-intensive to produce and uncomfortable to wear for any length of time. For these reasons, from some point in the late third, or perhaps early fourth centuries, the *lorica segmentata* fell out of favour as the armour of choice. From this time forward, Roman soldiers would typically wear either chain mail or scale mail armour and that in some instances, the individual pieces would be made from horn plates (Latin: *lamellae*). This offered far less protection to its wearer, but was cheaper, easier to maintain and could be produced in greater quantities much more rapidly: an essential when there was a larger standing army to equip. The large convex shield (Latin: *scutum*) was also replaced with a smaller, hoplite-like round or oval shield (Latin: *clipeus*) though the term *scutum* appears to have become a catch-all for any kind of shield by the time of the later Roman Empire.[26] This change appears to have occurred at some point during the third century. Helmets (Latin: *cassis*) were the one piece of defensive equipment that were upgraded: traditional cavalry helmets had offered more protection to the cheeks and neck than their infantry counterparts. During the third century, these improvements were implemented in the redesign of the infantry helmets.

The overall reduction in defensive equipment was not about cost cutting, however, nor was it an indication that the emperor thought the lives of frontier troops to be of lesser value than the Italians of the earlier legions. For a justification of the changes that were enacted, we should look back to the career of Alexander the Great.

Alexander, and his father Philip II, fundamentally changed Greek warfare. Traditionally, Greek battles had been fought by hoplites who were heavily armoured and carried a relatively short thrusting spear. Alexander (or Philip) fundamentally changed this system by introducing a far longer spear (sarissa) and significantly reducing the defensive armour that these *pezhetairoi* (from the Greek; translated as 'foot soldiers' and specific to Alexander and the Hellenistic period) wore. This had the effect of increasing the offensive capability of the infantry units by having several rows of spear heads projecting from the front of the formation. It also increased the manoeuvrability and the speed at which the troops could move because they were much less encumbered. This meant that they could march at a far greater rate each day and thus cover more ground. For the Romans, this innovation was highly desirable for the defence of the Empire (and as we have seen, trouble could increasingly flare up at different points widely spaced out across the frontiers) whereas for Alexander it was desirable because he wanted to be able to take his enemies by surprise. In both cases, the effect of increased flexibility of movement was the same.

On another interesting parallel, Alexander also made far greater use of cavalry than was traditional in Greek warfare, as did the Romans from this period. Roman armies of the fourth century were, therefore, a move in the direction of the great Macedonian army of Alexander the Great, of the fourth century BC.[27] Although it is interesting to note these similarities, we should be careful not to follow along this line of thinking too far, because a Roman soldier would still have been far more heavily defended with armour and a larger shield, and would also have had greater offensive capability through the *plumbatae*, and throwing spear. This Roman move in the direction of greater operational effectiveness was certainly not a deliberate attempt to imitate Alexander's army.

Outside of the directly offensive and defensive military equipment (in Latin, the general term for weaponry and associated military equipment is: *arma*), the clothing of a Roman soldier also changed. Traditional Roman clothing had been manufactured in Italy, but the majority of military activity now took place in the rather colder climates of central and northern Europe: warmer clothing was required. To meet this need, a long sleeved tunic was produced, as were trousers and socks. There was still the key piece of military garb: the *chlamys* (a military cloak). This adaptation was again a third century innovation, and was eventually increasingly adopted in the warmer climates as well as the colder ones once the practicality of trousers and socks was more widely recognised.[28]

To turn to the standard issue kit, or *arma*, for a regular soldier, this included items such as a blanket, a water bottle, enough rations to last at least three days and possibly for up to as much as twenty days in order that they did not need constant resupplying while on campaign, spare clothes and any other personal items he may wish to carry with him, besides the expected uniform, weaponry and armour. From the evidence of a soldier's will in 320, we find that a soldier may have also been expected to carry a hatchet, a sack, a saddlebag, a bronze table and bronze measuring cup. These items would combine to a weight of around 25kg, though some extra kit items (such as those necessary for making temporary shelters) may not have been carried by the soldier but by the baggage train animals.

These bare bones lists do not quite give us a sense of what it might have been like on the ground; if we wish to imagine more fully the day-to-day realities of life in the army, the Theodosian Code again proves useful. On the quality of a soldier's food rations, for example:

> Study of past practice has revealed that our soldiers, during the time of a campaign, are accustomed to receive hard tack and bread, ordinary wine and also sour wine, and meat, both pork and mutton, as follows: hard tack for two days out of three, bread on the third day; ordinary wine on one day, sour wine on the other; pork for one day out of three, mutton on the other two days.[29]

The reality of surviving on a limited diet such as this (though *garum*, or fish sauce, a Roman speciality, was also popular with soldiers) reminds us both of the small scale but also represents something of the large. Firstly, the life of a soldier was undoubtedly a hard one, and on the individual level, living hand-to-mouth in this way would have been what being in the army was really all about and how it was experienced. However, this source also reveals the extent of the logistical and tactical thinking behind this kind of careful rationing from the perspective of the individual. Naturally, this kind of thought and preparation was necessary, since it was of course a major logistical challenge to equip, supply and move around the entire Roman army and one which could not have happened had it not been organised and managed in advance exactly how much meat, wine and bread each individual soldier would actually get. As always, Vegetius has something instructive to say on the massively important, expensive and laborious logistical challenge that was feeding the Roman army:

> The order of subjects demands that I speak next about the provisioning system for fodder and grain. For armies are more often destroyed by starvation than battle, and hunger is more savage than the sword. Secondly, other misfortunes can in time be alleviated: fodder and grain supply have no remedy in a crisis except storage in advance.
>
> On any expedition the single most effective weapon is that food should be sufficient for you while dearth should break the enemy. Therefore, before war is commenced, careful consideration should be given to supplies and their issue in order that fodder, grain and the other army provisions customarily requisitioned from provincials may be exacted in good time, and quantities always more than sufficient be assembled at points well-placed for waging war and well-fortified.
>
> But if the taxes in kind be insufficient, everything (needed) should be compulsorily purchased from advance payments in gold. For there is no secure possession of wealth, unless it be maintained by defence of arms.[30]

In conclusion, the Roman soldiers of the fourth century would have looked different in some regards from their first century counterparts. However, many individual items would have been the same or similar (the helmet, for example) and the basic components of shield, sword and so forth certainly remained the same, as did the types of standard kit soldiers carried , such as a water bottle or blanket.

The Frontiers

There was never one single blueprint for the composition of the various frontiers of the Roman Empire. The frontiers could be defined by a continuous wall, a road, a river or a series of watch towers. Nor did the frontiers have a single purpose. We can say with some certainty that they likely were not intended to be an impenetrable barrier to invasion from a foreign power. No road (like the *limes*), no series of watch towers or fortifications could ever prevent a determined invasion by even a modest army. The *limitanei* were also too spread out to resist any invasion for long. So what were the frontiers really about, if not preventing outside attack?

In reality the frontiers had a number of functions: some military, some civil. They were certainly intended to have a measure of defensive function, although (as noted) the *limitanei* were probably not of sufficient strength to fight off a serious invasion, they would have been able to resist small-scale raiding parties. The frontiers would also have acted as a deterrent to some potential invaders: the line of watch towers or similar would have essentially worked as a potent and very real symbol of Roman might. Relatively weak and loosely structured, untrained or untested raiding bands made up of discontents of all stripes from outside of the Empire would certainly have been put off by such an effective symbol, but the symbolism may well have been exactly the reverse for more powerful tribes. They would have seen the Roman Empire as being wealthy and ripe for raiding, if not conquest, as demonstrated by the well-constructed watch towers. The frontiers would also have acted as a form of border control, helping to account for the flow of trade both into and out of the Empire.

Perhaps most importantly of all, the frontiers would have acted as a very real demarcation for the Romans of the limits of their empire. If there had been sign posts on the frontier they could have read: *ne plus ultra* (thus far and no further). The frontier did help to form a hinterland between the Empire and what was not-Roman that lay beyond, but it was certainly not a hard barrier and the Roman sphere of influence naturally extended beyond the frontier, through connections such as trade links and the spread of Latin as a lingua franca, just as influences from outside came in.

The third-century crisis was wide-ranging and extensive in its reach: it was a nexus of political, cultural and financial transformations, to say nothing of the military and warfare changes already discussed. As part of the military crisis, there was the collapse of the northern frontier. Small-scale raids across the Rhine and Danube frontiers gave way to larger-scale invasions. During the mid-third century there is considerable archaeological evidence for the destruction of many Roman forts along this frontier area, although exactly who destroyed them is open to discussion. No doubt some would have been destroyed at the hands of invading tribes, and some could well have been destroyed during the many internecine struggles of the period; either way the efficiency of the frontier system certainly collapsed in the northern empire. The empire retreated from some frontiers, and even the entire province of Dacia was abandoned.

After these great changes, gradually, during the second half of the third century, the situation was resolved and new fortified frontier zones were established. The Saxon shore forts were built in Britain. The *limes* on the Rivers Danube and Rhine was strengthened. Forts were reconstructed and troops were permanently positioned in the frontier areas.[31] Diocletian increased significantly the number of legions, although these were generally much smaller so the overall impact on the size of the army is unclear. Diocletian also reorganised the defence of the Danube region, in particular designing a new style of watch tower, of which several were built along that frontier.

It is difficult to establish with a degree of certainty what reforms Constantine was responsible for in terms of frontier policy. He could easily have been responsible for the construction of several forts on the 'barbarian' side of the Rhine and Danube, which would have represented a more aggressive Roman posture. Instead of reacting to invasion and aggression from outside, Rome began to make occasional pre-emptive raids across the frontier to keep their enemies on the back foot, and to send a powerful message that the empire was still a military force to be reckoned with.

The situation on the eastern frontier was rather different. A state of either open warfare or a very strained peace (of the: 'they make a desert and they call it peace' type) existed between the Roman Empire and that of Parthia/ Persia for the whole of the third and fourth centuries. The third century saw many wars and many campaigns in the east. Rome was often successful and captured Ctesiphon more than once. Rome also created two new provinces in the east during Septimius Severus' campaign of 197. Roman campaigns often took them beyond the River Tigris, but they never attempted to annex territory this far east. They were perhaps realistic enough to know that they had little chance of holding it, so these invasions were a show of strength more than wars of conquest to capture and keep new land.

Despite Roman successes, the Persians also made occasional gains. In 252, for example, Syria, Mesopotamia and Cappadocia were invaded by Shapur, the Persian king.[32] This shows how the frontier in the east was under constant threat and frequently changed hands. Successive Roman emperors evidently realised the strategic importance of campaigns in the east and typically commanded them personally (though this was not always either wise or successful). Later, the frontier in the east established by Septimius Severus was a fortified road running from Damascus to Palmyra. At various periods Rome commanded more territory than that, depending on whether the pendulum of victory had swung their way over the highly disputed eastern frontier, but during the reign of Diocletian this was taken to be the limits of empire. As a consequence, forts further inside Roman territory were abandoned and new fortified towers were built all down this road.[33]

To summarise: the story of the eastern frontier is one of continuous warfare with Rome sometimes on top, and sometimes on the defensive. Neither power ever seems to have had the strength, or perhaps drive, to destroy the other in such a way that would end the invasions for good. However, and even despite the constant warfare, it could be argued that the northern frontier was more dangerous exactly because of its unpredictability, and because of the unprecedented threat level of barbarian invasion.

Chapter 4

Turin and Verona

If Constantine's military success rested on the army he commanded, then it is no less the case that it also partly rested on his personal tactical genius, partly on the fact that he was not a man to underestimate the importance of intelligence in the art of war. A tenth century source (obviously well after Constantine's own time, but with a description that reads realistically enough to make it credible) makes this clear for us:

> When he [Constantine] was intending to go on an expedition, Constantine the Great was accustomed to take counsel with those who had experience in the relevant matters, such as where and when the expedition should be undertaken. When he had ascertained from this advice the place and time for the expedition, he was also accustomed to enquire as to which others knew about these matters, particularly those with recent experience. And when he had found whether any others were knowledgeable, he summoned these also and asked each one individually how long the route was which ran from home territory to the objective, and of what sort; and whether one road or many led to the objective; and whether the regions along the route were waterless or not. And he then enquired as to which road was narrow, precipitous and dangerous, and which broad and traversable; also whether there was any great river along the way which could not be crossed. Next he enquired about the country: how many fortresses it possessed, which were secure and which insecure, which populous and which sparsely populated, what distance these fortresses were from one another; and of what sort were the villages about them, large or small, and whether these regions were level or rough, grassy or arid. He asked this on account of fodder for the horses. He then enquired about which army was available to support these fortresses in time of war.[1]

Constantine was the kind of man who knew he had to prepare ahead to win, and that good intelligence was the key to success; this was even more the case in the campaign year 311/12 which was a pivotal one in the reign of Constantine. In April of 311 Galerius was on his deathbed, believing that his illness was inflicted upon him by the God of the Christians as retribution for his persecution of them. Not only was Galerius fatally ill, but his most recent persecution of the Christians had failed. Galerius' final act on the political stage was to issue an edict of toleration of Christians. Some have argued that this was an attempt to remove any political responsibility from his successors for his persecutions, but it is perhaps just as likely that he hoped his illness would be miraculously cured: it was not and he died on the road to Romulianum, his place of birth, on the Danube with Licinius in attendance.[2]

Throughout Roman history, the death of a leading political figure had immediate consequences, and this was no different. In the east, Maximinus grabbed control of Asia Minor before anyone else could react. He then remitted all taxation from the citizenry of those provinces, essentially buying their support and good will.[3] Licinius responded in a similar vein, offering a reduction in tax liabilities for serving and retired soldiers in the east. After securing the loyalty of his troops, Licinius moved against Maximinus. War in the eastern provinces looked inevitable, but neither commander felt able to press home an advantage, and an uneasy treaty was signed on board a ship.

The alliance of Maximinus and Licinius put Constantine in a potentially difficult position: if these two were to come to an arrangement with Maxentius as well, then Constantine would be outnumbered and overmatched militarily. Constantine likely saw war as inevitable, and ever the consummate politician and deal-broker; he contracted a marriage alliance with Licinius. Constantine offered Licinius the hand of his sister, Constantia, which Licinius duly accepted. This newly-formed alliance essentially broke the brief and shaky treaty between Licinius and Maximinus and drove the latter and Maxentius into each other's willing arms. These political machinations set the stage for the campaign of 312: Constantine would go to war with Maxentius in the west and Licinius would oppose Maximinus in the east. This strategic marriage was politically vital to Constantine; he needed Licinius as an ally, firstly to keep Maximinus busy in the east, but also to threaten Maxentius' flanks in the west. More than this, however, Constantine needed to keep Licinius busy; he could not allow Licinius to conquer Italy as this would seriously impair Constantine's own imperial aspirations.

The year 311 ended with Maxentius denying Constantine's imperial credentials and even destroying statues of him in Gaul. Outright war was not yet declared, but it seemed fairly inevitable once the winter had passed and final preparations were made. The campaign of 312 began with a formal declaration of war between the western opponents. Constantine was still in his winter quarters at Trier and Maxentius stationed himself at Verona in north-eastern Italy in anticipation of a flanking attack from Licinius that never materialised; the latter was more intent on acquiring Asia Minor from Maximinus.

With Maxentius firmly fixed in place by the threat of Licinius, Constantine marched directly south from Trier to Vienne, no doubt asking the kinds of questions necessary to a successful campaign as outlined in the source at the beginning of the chapter. From there he turned east and headed towards northern Italy; once across the Alps he was in the territory of Maxentius and there was no turning back: *alea iacta est*. Constantine was marching quickly, perhaps unsure how long Maxentius would remain at Verona once it became clear that Licinius was not interested in Italy, but just as likely it was out of a desire to take Maxentius by surprise, and, with any luck, not fully prepared for war.

The first organised resistance to Constantine in Italy was at the town of Segusium (modern Susa). This was a fortified and well-defended position that remained loyal to Maxentius even as Constantine bore down on them. Constantine could not afford the time a formal and well-planned siege could take, especially with Maxentius' army 'larger in manpower' so close by. Nor did he possess a siege train that was close enough to assist with the capture of a well-defended town. Yet Constantine's strategy could not allow a hostile position to remain on his lines of supply and communication when battle with Maxentius looked imminent. Constantine had little option but to take a gamble; he ordered the gates set on fire and the walls stormed with only scaling ladders. This was a non-standard sledge hammer approach to a siege that was taken out of necessity. For Constantine, the gamble paid off.

The gates of the town quickly caught fire and as Constantine's troops began to gain the walls, the defenders sued for peace. In ancient warfare, this would typically have been far too late to save the defenders from the ravages inflicted upon them by a successful army. Constantine had no wish to exact a toll upon the defenders, however, so he ordered a halt to the assault and further ordered his troops to put out the fires they had started lest they spread to the rest of the town. In doing this, Constantine wanted to be seen as a liberator and the rightful ruler rather than a savage and brutal conqueror of Italy, out for rapine and booty at any cost. This episode also illustrates very clearly the discipline of the Roman legionaries. They immediately stopped a siege at the height of its prosecution upon receiving orders from their superiors; not only this but they turned their attentions to saving the town. Clearly, this demonstrates the professionalism and slick functioning of a military force who were there to do what they were told, not to break out, smash and grab at the first opportunity.

Having secured his lines of supply and communication, Constantine believed that the main defensive hub of north-western Italy, Augusta Taurinorum (modern Turin), lay open to him. Turin is around 30 miles east of Susa and lies in a naturally strong defensive position at the Dora and Po Rivers: not for naught was it seen as the gateway to Italy if approaching from Gaul, which is what Constantine was doing.[4]

While Constantine had been busying himself marching into Italy and capturing Susa, Maxentius had not been idle. He had abandoned (or more accurately left a small maintenance force) at Verona in case Licinius' strategy changed, and had marched directly west to meet Constantine at Turin. Maxentius took up a position west of Turin in a great plain, and awaited Constantine's arrival. He did not have to wait long. Constantine's strategy of allying himself with Licinius in order to pin Maxentius in position had not been a total success, but had worked well enough to allow Constantine to cross the Alps unopposed, which was all he really needed.

Maxentius was a difficult opponent for Constantine. He was no military genius, but was at least capable. However, he did possess a vastly superior army, numbering around 100,000 men. In order to put such a large force in the field, Maxentius must have called together virtually every soldier he had at his disposal, less a few to defend key strategic sites such as Verona. Constantine on the other hand had a much larger territorial area to defend. He could not denude Gaul of troops in order to prosecute his campaign against Maxentius. The Rhine border still had to be defended, and significant numbers of troops were left in this region. At Turin, Constantine commanded not more than 40,000, something like a quarter of his total order of battle. The writer of the Latin Panegyric states that the army which Alexander the Great commanded at the Hellespont was 40,000, this being the ideal number to maintain flexibility and manoeuvrability, he further states that Constantine commanded fewer men than this:

> Although Alexander the Great could impose an unlimited levy upon all of Greece and the whole of Illyricum in addition to his own Macedonians, he never led out more than forty thousand men, since he considered that anything in excess of that was unwieldy for the commander and a mob rather than an army. But you with even fewer numbers embarked upon a much greater war, since your own virtue made you as much more powerful as his greater numbers made him better prepared.[5]

Not unaware of the difference in numbers, and in order to meet this challenge, Constantine had been on a recruitment drive, and in line with usual practice, had raised an army before the campaign in order to bring the numbers closer to requirements. He recruited men especially from Gaul and Germany, and as discussed many of his units (such as *auxilia palatina*) were majority non-Roman, though these types of units were not spread throughout the entire army in a uniform fashion. As Zosimus records: '[Constantine was] levying troops from the barbarians he had conquered and the Germans and the other Gauls, together with those collected from Britain.'[6]

It is not clear in the sources how long Maxentius had been waiting at Turin for Constantine, but it was long enough for him to be rested and already set up on the battlefield waiting for his opponent to finish with Susa and advance to meet him. Maxentius could not have known with certainty that Constantine would move against Turin after his capture of Susa, but it was an educated guess. He would have reasoned that Constantine would want to secure the fortifications leading into Italy before progressing further, especially with Maxentius' hostile force close by.

Constantine would have been aware of Maxentius' position on the plain from scouting reports, and he would have known that the army opposing his entry into Italy was around twice the size of his own. He had little choice but to fight a battle, however. Retreat would have been strategically and politically disastrous, and moving into Italy leaving Maxentius to his rear would have been suicidal. A battle was therefore inevitable.

We know a little of the order of battle for each side; from a Latin Panegyric we have the mention that Maxentius commanded a number of heavily armed, mailed cavalry who were termed *clibanarii* (though they were also known as *cataphracti*; this latter is a Latinisation of the Greek *kataphraktos*, the Latin equivalent is *loricatus* – mailed – whence *lorica*):

> What a spectacle that is said to have been, how dreadful to behold, how terrible, horses and men alike enclosed in a covering of iron! In the army they are called *clibanarii*: the men are covered [with mail] in the upper part, a corselet which extends down to the horses' chests and hands to their forelegs protects them from the injury of a wound without impeding their gait.[7]

Amusingly, the term *clibanarii* is itself thought to derive from the Latin *clibanus*; a type of iron oven. This etymology rather bluntly conveys how fearsomely the *clibanarii* must have come across, and so understandably these *cataphracti* were the cream of the troops Maxentius had available to him, though heavily-mailed cavalry were not a totally new sight for the Romans, despite the panegyricist's suggestion as such. As the same source relates, they were heavily armoured in mail shirts, as were their horses, who were themselves also partly armoured. They were an outstanding shock weapon when used correctly, and from their positioning in Maxentius' line he was evidently well aware of this:

> Their [the *clibanarii*] training for combat is to preserve the course of their assault after they have crashed into opposing line, and since they are invulnerable they resolutely break through whatever is set against them.[8]

Reconstructing this battle is a little difficult, but continuing to draw on the panegyricist we learn how Constantine responded to the fearsomely iron-clad cavalry that Maxentius had presented:

> But you, most prudent Emperor, who knew all the ways of fighting, got assistance from your ingenuity: that it is safest to elude those whom it is most difficult to withstand [it therefore appears that Constantine did not himself have any *clibanarii*]. By drawing your lines apart you induce an enemy attack which cannot be reversed; next by leading your lines back together you hem in the men whom you admit to your game. It did them no good to press forward, since your men purposely gave way; iron's rigidity did not allow a change in direction for pursuit.[9]

It seems that the downside of the *clibanarii* was their relative lack of manoeuvrability, and that Constantine had enough insight to see this and make best use of it for his own advantage. In comparison, regarding Maxentius' line, the Latin Panegyric tells us:

> The enemy [Maxentius' troops] were now widely spread out in a disorganised manner so that they were easily cut down while dispersed.[10]

There is no reason to suppose that Maxentius' troops would have been widely dispersed (and the panegyricist has a reason to play down Maxentius' preparedness and battle savvy). Surely Roman discipline, which as we know was exacting, would not have allowed for this. This statement does tell us, however, that he was at least expecting a battle and was already in position to receive Constantine's advances. The Latin Panegyric goes on to tell us:

> Their battle line [Maxentius'] was arrayed in the form of a wedge with their flanks extending downhill to the rear, and if you

[Constantine] had eagerly joined battle with them at the outset, they would have turned back and surrounded your men as they were engaged in fighting.[11]

This is an interesting statement; it tells us a number of important pieces of information. Firstly that the plain on which the battle was fought was not entirely flat; there must have been at least one small hill (hence 'downhill') upon which Maxentius has set up his troops. Secondly it tells us that Maxentius most likely did completely occupy the top of the hill. In ancient warfare, the occupation of the high ground was usually considered critical to the success of the battle; with 100,000 men, even if they were standing very close together, and many deep, the line would still be several miles long. Thus, Maxentius was probably occupying the whole of the hill, even if it were a large one, and still with enough of his troops left over to have the flanks refused downhill. Thirdly, the translation 'turned back' (from the Latin: *reflexa*) connotes an outflanking manoeuvre, and this implies that Maxentius intended to execute this by his positioning.

So Maxentius' line was a convex shape (from the perspective of the enemy facing), a crescent with the heavy cavalry at the apex and the wings sweeping backwards. His troops must have been set quite deep. Perhaps Maxentius did not want to extend his line beyond the slopes of the hill, and used the extra troops to reinforce the apex of his central wedge. His intention being obvious enough: to drive the wedge through Constantine's centre, divide the enemy force in two and then wheel left and right to slaughter each half independently. A reasonable enough tactic, and certainly an innovation over the more usual encirclement trap employed when one army had the superior manpower. But the Latin Panegyric also hints at a secondary plan of Maxentius:

If you had eagerly joined battle with them at the outset, they would have turned and surrounded your men as they were engaged in fighting.[12]

Maxentius, then, had a two-fold plan. If Constantine were to attack him directly by opening the battle, then Maxentius would attempt an envelopment. If Constantine allowed Maxentius to open the battle, then Maxentius would drive his cavalry through the Constantinian centre. Given the positioning of the cavalry in the centre, it seems very likely that Maxentius preferred to take the battle initiative and smash Constantine's forces with his *cataphracti*.

Maxentius probably thought that he would surprise Constantine with these tactics, and likely he would have done if not for the fact that Maxentius was set up in formation as Constantine arrived on the field of battle. This they were, and Constantine's scouting parties had performed their job admirably. Good intelligence being everything in warfare, he was well aware of the positioning of Maxentius' forces, and quickly discerned from this Maxentius' tactical plan: to concentrate his forces against the centre of Constantine's line, smashing Constantine's forces decisively. Constantine was also well aware of the size of the enemy forces, and that they were drawn up in a convex shape. To counter this, Constantine drew up his own forces in a concave shape with the cavalry apparently stationed on his wings. This formation invited Maxentius to implement his plan of attacking his enemy at the centre.

Maxentius seemingly had also deployed men in forests to either side of what would be the route of Constantine's advance. These men would have been stationed with the intention of ambushing the passing troops, or more likely aiding in the battle by launching a flanking attack at an opportune moment. Therefore, in order to produce the opposite formation to the one adopted by Maxentius, Constantine's wings advanced more rapidly than the centre initially. The scouts had evidently also seen the ambush parties and these forward wings flushed them out before any damage could be done.

Constantine's army finally came to a halt at the base of the hill, his wings arrayed further forward of the infantry in the centre in a concave shape. Maxentius' troops on the top of the hill were in the opposite convex formation. Once the two armies were in position, neither commander had to wait long for the battle to be joined. Maxentius took the initiative and ordered his mailed cavalry forward. As noted earlier, these were in the very centre of his line, and therefore were the furthest forward of Maxentius' entire army. They charged straight down the hill right at Constantine's centre, as per their orders and the tactical plan.

From the Latin Panegyric, it seems that Constantine had deliberately weakened his centre in anticipation of Maxentius' attack. As soon as the *cataphracti* reached Constantine's centre, the infantry stationed there melted away into the infantry formations to either side, and the heavy cavalry charged ineffectually straight through the resulting gap in the enemy line, as recorded by the panegyricist above.[13]

So it seems that what Maxentius had hoped for was a decisive strike against Constantine's centre. His cavalry would then have been given the orders to outflank Constantine's centre by attacking from both their right and left. Maxentius would have thus anticipated a fight that would have allowed his infantry time to reach the enemy and stream through the anticipated gap straight after their cavalry and so provide fighting support to the flanking attacks. But from the Latin Panegyric as quoted, this is not what happened. Constantine's orders to allow the mailed cavalry through unopposed was a master stroke, and strongly reminiscent of Alexander the Great's genius move to make a way for Darius' scythed chariots to pass unhindered through the Macedonian lines, to be swiftly dealt with by skirmishers stationed behind them.

As per Constantine's expectations, Maxentius' cavalry went straight through the Constantinian lines almost before they knew what had happened; they could never have anticipated such a quick (and unopposed) break-through. Before they could reform from their charge and execute the final phase of their orders (the flanking attack against the infantry to both sides) Constantine's cavalry came streaming from both wings and executed their own flanking attack against their more heavily armoured opponents, but before the *cataphracti* had time to turn about and relying on their own confusion and disarray. This was Constantine's tactic all along; he had armed his cavalry with specially made clubs with metal heads that his cavalry used to batter the life out of their more heavily armed (but their Achilles' heel was that they were far less manoeuvrable) opponents. These were unable to reform in time to face down Constantine's cavalry once they had been allowed through, and were perplexed by this unexpected turn of events:

> Thus our men assailed those who were delivered to them with clubs equipped with heavy iron knobs which wore out an invulnerable enemy with their beating, and when they were inflicted especially on their heads they forced those whom the blows had confused to tumble down. Then they began to fall headlong, to slide down backward, to totter half-dead or dying to be held fast by their saddles, to lie entangled in the confused slaughter of horses, which in unbridled pain, when their vulnerable points had been discovered, cast their riders everywhere.[14]

In this way, the mailed cavalry were quickly and decisively removed from the battle before they had even had much of a chance to do any damage at all. The Constantinian centre soon reformed after it had so quickly deliberately melted away; another superb indication of the quality and discipline of Roman troops. Once they had reformed, Constantine ordered his infantry to advance and because of the shape of the two formations he began to envelop the larger enemy force. The ease with which the mailed cavalry (clearly intended by Maxentius to be his crack troops) had been dispatched had an understandably depressive impact on morale. The defenders gave ground and the wings were driven back towards each other. The greater manpower of Maxentius was irrelevant in this case as many of the Romans were trapped in the centre and could not come to grips with the enemy. Maxentius' troops were constantly giving ground and being pressed ever harder on their flanks, and finally they broke and ran from the field. Typically, this marks the occasion in a Roman battle where the greatest slaughter occurred. Constantine's cavalry would have therefore been particularly busy in mopping up the slowest to retreat.

Maxentius had initially taken up a position to the west of Turin, a town which nominally he held, and so this was the natural place for the defeated army to retreat towards, take up their position there and prepare for a siege. The battle had occurred very close to the town, however, and the citizens and city elders had been watching proceedings from the fortifications. They had seen how Constantine had outwitted and easily defeated the forces of Maxentius and they made a rapid and expedient decision to switch allegiances. They quickly closed their gates to the retreating Roman troops. The Romans evidently did not initially realize this and they still fled to the gates of the city, expecting to gain the temporary safety of the Turin defences. In the Latin Panegyric we have a description of the situation:

> They were routed and cut down right up to the walls of Turin, and when they reached the gates already fastened by the inhabitants they closed them off as well by the mass of their own bodies.[15]

Inevitably, Constantine's forces chased the retreating Romans and trapped them against the walls of Turin; the slaughter was cheered along by the citizens of the town who were watching from the battlements.[16] After the fighting was over, the gates of Turin were opened to Constantine and another key strategic holding was taken without further incident. Maxentius (along with what remnants there were of his army) fled back towards Verona to rejoin with the fresh troops he had left behind to guard his flanks. From there, Maxentius appears to have travelled south before Constantine arrived to follow up his victory.

After the surrender of Turin, Constantine followed Maxentius eastwards, determined to force matters to a conclusion. He first of all moved northeast towards Milan. News of his victory, and his lenient treatment (with the proviso of their surrender) of both Susa and Turin, persuaded many towns and cities in northern Italy to send envoys offering their allegiance. Before he arrived at the gates of Milan, Constantine had already accepted its surrender and he was welcomed into the city with open arms as its liberator: the very image favourable to himself which he was desperate to portray. Milan had suffered a significant loss of status while Maxentius ruled in Rome, and the city's welcome of Constantine was in all likelihood perfectly genuine. There is a description of the scene in the Latin Panegyric:

What a day that was when you entered Milan! What rejoicing there was among the chief men of the city, what applause of the populace! What security there was for mothers and maidens gazing at you, and what a twofold delight they enjoyed, when they looked upon the form of a most beautiful Emperor and feared no licence! They all displayed themselves and danced about without any apprehension about the remainder of the war; they counted the beginning of your victory as consummation: it seemed that it was not the Transpadane provinces [that part of Cisalpine Gaul between the River Padus (River Po) and the Alps] which had been recovered, but Rome.[17]

Naturally, Constantine's forces were battle-sore: they had had a long march from Trier and had fought a difficult, albeit often overlooked, battle just outside Turin. He now took the opportunity to rest his army in Milan (though for a period of time unknown to the modern historian) during high summer, thus enabling them time to rest as well as allowing for the possibility of troop replacements to be brought in from Gaul.

Though this is not to suggest that Constantine was resting on his laurels; despite Constantine's successes, he knew that Maxentius remained in a strong position and in possession of two large garrisons: one at Verona, commanded by Pompeianus, and the other on the Adriatic coast not far away. If Constantine's ambition was to be realised, he still had to defeat Maxentius once and for all, and thereby take possession of the whole of Italy.

The panegyricist records what happens once Constantine left Milan:

'Why should I relate, after so great and serious a battle, that at Brescia a band of cavalry, large enough and eager, but feeling safer in flight than in its own power, was repulsed at your first onslaught and sped as far as Verona for more assistance? Not that it was a disgrace, because those who yield to you are excused in the running away. On the contrary, that wretched cowardice may attain something to boast of, a flight which had dignity.'[18]

Constantine did not delay his advance and continued his direct march towards Verona and Maxentius' garrison there. The city of Verona was brilliantly sited. It was built in a bend in the River Adige and was located there specifically because of its strategic importance and potential for defensive capability. The River Adige flows south from the Alps to the north towards the western side of the city; there it bends back on itself and goes round the outskirts of Verona, before draining into the Adriatic. The description of the River Adige in the Latin Panegyric is as follows:

> The River Adige, rough and stony, full of eddies and whirlpools, with its fierce current prevented any assault and rendered all the region behind it safe and secure from penetration of enemy forces.[19]

Verona, therefore, was protected on three sides by this fast-flowing river, and on the final fourth by a large wall constructed by Gallienus. There was also a single bridge over the river, but this could be easily defended in the event of a concerted assault. All these conditions made the city a fortress, constructed with the specific aim in mind of being a bastion against invasion from the north.

Since he had been waging wars elsewhere, Constantine did not have the engineering capability with him to carry out a siege of the city immediately. However, he could not advance on Italy while still leaving a strong Maxentian force to his rear, so his only option was to invest the city. There were only two ways out for the defenders: across the wall to the south or over the bridge to the north. Constantine needed to block both points of ingress and egress. Constantine assumed that if a breakout was to be attempted, it would likely come through the gate in the southern wall. He therefore moved the main body of his army to the south of the city to blockade it from the south. He also sent a much smaller detachment of light infantry into the foothills of the Alps to find a crossing point. Once this was discovered, these troops moved into the plain to the north to prevent the defenders escaping across the bridge. The northern detachment was small because he realized he could reinforce it fairly quickly if required.

Constantine could not force entry into the city because he lacked the siege equipment, but his smaller army could be supplied from the local region. This allowed him to blockade the city easily and so starve out the defenders. Maxentius' garrison in the city was large, far too large to survive a siege for long: water was not a problem, but food would quickly run out. When he had moved south before Constantine arrived, Maxentius had left a Praetorian Prefect, Ruricius Pompeianus, in charge of the garrisons of the region. Immediately grasping the severity of the situation for the defenders, and before the blockade was complete to the south, Pompeianus marched out to attack Constantine's troops. The purpose of this sally was not to break the blockade, or to destroy the besieging army; rather it was to allow Pompeianus to escape with a small detachment of troops through Constantine's lines. The attackers, the sallying troops, were quickly driven back into the city; the attack was evidently not a full scale one, but it did achieve its objective. Pompeianus escaped the besieged city and rode eastwards to bring back reinforcements and attempt to lift the siege.[20]

Pompeianus returned after what was in all likelihood only a few days, with a large force consisting of most of the troops that Maxentius had stationed in northern Italy. Constantine's position was now serious. He was besieging the city to his north with the ever-present threat of a breakout attempt from that sector. He was also faced with being completely surrounded by the newly-arrived army to his south.

In the Latin Panegyric there is praise reserved for Constantine for not allowing Pompeianus to interrupt the siege, which proceeded as before. Constantine actually took the decision to divide his force. He left the smallest part behind to continue the siege, although in reality this was only a holding force to prevent an attack to his rear from the city when he was engaged in fighting the newly-arrived troops. Therefore, it was the bulk of his army which he led as he turned away from the city and marched to meet Pompeianus. The Latin Panegyric again:

> You preferred to engage him [Pompeianus] with lesser forces upon his return rather than to interrupt the siege, so the men shut in could neither recover their strength nor escape nor threaten your rear.[21]

This passage implies that if Constantine had broken the siege, the two armies would have been perhaps equal in size. It continues in the Latin Panegyric:

> At first, I hear, you had drawn up a double battle line; next when you had discerned the number of the enemy you ordered the ranks to spread out in front of the army to be extended more widely, estimating of course the spirit of all your men on the basis of your own, that a mass however much heavier could be broken by the attack of fewer men.[22]

Constantine's initial double line probably had more to do with the limitations of space on the battlefield, until he was a few hundred metres from his siege camp, than any miscalculation on his part of the size of the enemy contingent.

We know little of the actual course of the battle, save that in the Latin Panegyric, Constantine is berated for being in the thick of the fighting, at great risk to his own life:

> You had foreseen everything, you had arranged the whole, you had fulfilled the duty of the supreme commander: why did you enter the fray yourself, why did you thrust yourself into the densest throng of the enemy, why did you send the State's salvation into such great danger? Or do you think that we are unaware that,

while you were seized by excessive ardour, you arrived in the
midst of the enemy's weapons, and if you had not opened a path
for yourself by slaughter you had cheated the expectation and
prayers of the entire human race?[23]

Later on, it is suggested that a prepared position on a nearby hill may have
been more sensible, as with Xerxes watching the Battle of Salamis in 480.[24]
However, the advantage of Constantine's risk-taking behaviour was that his
presence in the thick of the fighting was very inspirational to his troops, and
they drove inexorably towards the figure of Pompeianus. They evidently
thought that to cut off the head of the snake was to kill the monster outright.
Pompeianus died during the fighting, although there is no evidence that
it was at Constantine's hands, or else the Panegyricist would have felt
incapable of ignoring this significant fact. As expected, once Pompeianus
was killed his army disappeared off in defeat.

The garrison at Verona watched the defeat in horror, unable to intervene.
When the relief army was defeated, they knew that with it went all their hope
of the siege being broken. By this time their food would have been low, but
their will to resist had certainly expired. They surrendered to Constantine
shortly after Pompeianus' death on the battlefield. The news of the latest
Constantinian victory quickly spread, and offers of surrender soon began
to arrive from every city in northern Italy; by the middle of October,
Constantine was the unquestioned ruler of northern Italy and the road to
Rome lay outstretched before him. The one small thing that got in his way
was the fact that Maxentius was still alive and so could be considered a threat
to his continued ambition.[25]

Maxentius had positioned himself in Rome and had been hoping that
Pompeianus would solve his northern problem. When this plan failed,
Maxentius had no choice but to do battle again with Constantine directly.
This is exactly what Constantine would have hoped: as we have seen, his
army was not exactly well-equipped for a lengthy siege, and the fortifications
of Rome were far stronger than any of the northern Italian cities. We also
know that Maxentius had a ready supply of grain from North Africa, and
therefore would not be starved out of the capital very quickly. The decisive
battle was coming: but where and under what conditions would it be fought?

Chapter 5

The Milvian Bridge

After victory against Maxentius' northern outposts, the towns and cities had come over to Constantine without any further difficulties. His army was now at near full working strength, and his lines of supply were secure; there was nothing now stopping him from seeking out Maxentius for the final show down. With that in mind, at some time in the middle of October, Constantine marched south towards Rome. His army was both small and mobile enough that he could have reached the capital relatively quickly, but in fact his marching speed was positively pedestrian. There are very good reasons for this, but in order to discover them we need to look at Maxentius' position in a little more detail.

As we all know, 'good emperors' were typically those who treated the populace well, though ideally they needed to have other attributes besides crowd-pleasing (such as enough military capability to expand the empire and conquer new territory), it did really help their careers no end to be able to keep the citizenry of Rome safe, well-fed and at minimal levels of taxation. Maxentius did none of those things. His rule was unquestionably based upon the army and his own military strength, to the detriment of the necessity of bread and circuses to keep a disenfranchised urban poor distracted from their potential to wield any real power. Maxentius was far from popular amongst Roman citizens. This is another reason why Constantine had so little difficulty in capturing the towns and cities in northern Italy: Constantine was generally viewed by Romans as a better choice in comparison to Maxentius.

As noted earlier, Constantine did not possess a siege train of any size or quality. His only option at Susa, for example, was to set fire to the gates and use scaling ladders where he could. The walls of Rome were of an order of magnitude stronger than those of any normal small town in northern Italy. If they were defended by a significant number of troops, such as the number

Maxentius commanded, Rome became a formidable fortress. Constantine would have feared that Maxentius would simply close the gates of Rome and play to Constantine's major weakness: his inability to force a siege. Thus Maxentius could theoretically hold out in Rome for a significant period of time, given he had no difficulties with food or water, and he commanded a significant number of troops including the elite Praetorian Guard.

Maxentius decided not to follow this eminently sensible strategy of forcing a siege which Constantine did not have the ability to prosecute. Instead, he gathered together his available forces and marched north to meet Constantine on the field of battle. But why did he do this? It is true to claim that the Roman legions were not defensive in nature. It went against the Roman grain to shore themselves up inside a defensive position and there wait for the enemy to come to them, even when it was the most sensible military option. True the Roman army was primarily designed to attack, but Maxentius' decision was far more complex and not based on this simple fact, but rather on other reasons of his own.

It has been argued that Maxentius saw two major justifications for marching out to meet Constantine, and both were based upon omens. The first justification was that it was late in the month, and the day on which the Battle of the Milvian Bridge was ultimately fought (28 October) was the sixth anniversary of Maxentius' accession. He likely would have seen this impending anniversary as a positive omen and thus a propitious day upon which to force the momentous battle.

The second justification which encouraged Maxentius to leave the security of Rome was again based upon an omen. The Sibylline Books had apparently been consulted as to the best course of action, and it turned out that they had declared the 28 October to be the day on which the enemy of Rome would be defeated. Adding this prophecy to the fact that the very same day was the anniversary of Maxentius' accession, he would have believed in all probability that he could not fail to win victory. The enemy of Rome in this case, however, proved to be Maxentius himself.[1] Interestingly, this prophecy of the Sibylline Books is remarkably similar to the answer received by Croesus of Lydia from the Pythia when he was considering invading Persia. He was told that a great empire would fall: in both cases the prophecy was suitably misleading.

The major problem with the genre of prophecy is that it is often backcast: these two omens may well have been a fiction created by later historians who were trying to make some sense out of a seemingly very poor strategic decision, but we must also not underestimate the power of, and belief in, omens in the Roman world. This is a belief that we have no evidence to suggest Maxentius did not himself share.

Besides the spell 28 October held over Maxentius, there were also more grounded reasons for Maxentius' decision which are too often ignored. There is little doubt that Maxentius was not a popular ruler. His rule and authority were based upon his control of the military; it was not a rule based upon taking the populace with him. This can be clearly seen (as discussed) from the occasions when Constantine took possession of northern Italy without resistance from the civilian population. In the ancient world there were three main methods of carrying out a siege:

- Force (a direct assault)
- Starvation (a blockade to cut off supply lines)
- Betrayal (treachery on the part of some number of the besieged)

Constantine did not have the military capability of forcing a siege, and Maxentius would have been well aware of this from scouting reports and from Constantine's actions at Susa. It would have been extremely difficult, close to impossible, in fact, for Constantine to have starved out the garrison and so force a surrender. He would essentially have had to disrupt Maxentius' supply lines in North Africa for this tactic to have had a hope of succeeding. Corruption and the betrayal that results was an ever-present threat, especially during civil wars where there were always sympathies to be found for both sides among a civilian population. (Philip of Macedon was a master of exploiting this tactic to save himself the cost, in both lives and gold, of a difficult, lengthy siege.) Maxentius would have been aware that his rule was unpopular. When he visited the Circus Maximus, for example, the crowd saw him and started chanting pro-Constantine slogans. Given this unpopularity, he probably would have feared that those in the citizenry who opposed his rule may have been able to assist the besieging army in some way, and thus cause Rome to fall relatively easily. But whatever the reasons behind Maxentius' decision, be they fear of betrayal, belief in omens or a simple strategic mistake, Maxentius decided to form up his available troops and to march north to meet Constantine.

Constantine's pedestrian marching is now a little easier to understand. A lightning march, such as those made famous by Alexander the Great, was always intended to take the enemy by surprise and unprepared for battle (or siege). This was the opposite of what Constantine wanted. Even unprepared, Maxentius would have been more than capable, militarily at least, of resisting a siege by virtue of his superior strength in numbers. Constantine wanted – needed – Maxentius to march out of Rome and meet him on the field of battle. Constantine's saunter thus gave Maxentius every opportunity to do this, and Constantine's patient tactical planning ultimately paid off.

It is impossible to discuss the prelude to the Battle of the Milvian Bridge without also discussing Constantine's visionary experiences. According to the church historian Eusebius, Constantine was profoundly worried as he marched to meet Maxentius. He knew he was outnumbered by the enemy and that the omens were against him. Eusebius tells us:

> He regarded the resources of soldiers and military numbers as secondary, for he thought that without the aid of a god these could achieve nothing; and he said that what comes from a god's assistance is irresistible and invincible.[2]

Although Constantine's later career shows that he was not much of a theologian, he evidently thought long and hard about the nature of the gods. According to Eusebius, he apparently considered the religious leanings of those who had already fought and lost to Maxentius. He also considered the relative merits of monotheism against the more traditionally Roman poly-theistic world view. Eusebius goes on:

> He marshalled these arguments in his mind, and concluded that it was folly to go on with the vanity of the gods which do not exist, and to persist in error in the face of so much evidence, and he decided that he should venerate his father's god alone.[3]

With Constantine's decision to favour the God of the Christians made, he began to pray. He beseeched and implored God to show him a sign of divine favour. As Constantine prayed, Eusebius tells us that there appeared to him a 'most remarkable divine sign'.[4] Eusebius is happy to concede that if anyone other than Constantine had claimed to have seen this divine sign it would not have been believable, but that the emperor should be believed because not only was he the emperor, but he told the story directly to Eusebius (under oath) some years later. Eusebius relates the details of the vision, and he vouches that these were told to him by Constantine himself:

> About the time of the midday sun, when day was just turning, he said he saw with his own eyes, up in the sky, up in the sky and resting over the sun, a cross-shaped trophy formed from light, and a text attached to it that said 'by this conquer'.[5]

The tag 'by this conquer', often translated into Latin as: *in hoc signo vinces*, itself a rendering of the Greek: *en toutô nika* later became Constantine's motto. At the time of the vision, Constantine was not with the main body of the army, but was commanding a secondary column campaigning else-where as he marched broadly south. Eusebius is certain that not only did

Constantine see this vision, but the entire body of troops he had with him at the time did also (though presumably, this is on Constantine's word rather than on direct interviews with each and every soldier).

A sceptic would suggest that it seems terribly convenient that Constantine was away from the main body of his army, and with only a handpicked band of loyal soldiers, each of which could be relied upon for discretion, when he had his vision. It further seems like a significant risk in the first place for Constantine himself to be away from the main army with a small contingent while in enemy territory and with a large army close by, so we may wonder how true it was that Constantine was indeed separated from almost all the rest. On the other hand, Constantine is hardly the first (or last) person to have made a claim to signs, visions or wonders, and while the expediency of what he saw may be apparent to sceptics (he was clearly hyper-aware of how good for troop morale the support of the divine is) it is simply not possible to write off the entire event as 'just his overactive imagination' or worse, 'just his cool calculation', because to do so would be to invite the complex question of what exactly does constitute normal consciousness, and who decides what this is. This is why the sequence of events surrounding his experience needs some analysis, which is as follows.

According to Eusebius, upon beholding the vision in the sky Constantine did not straightaway fully understand what he had seen, so he halted his column and meditated on the issue for some time. Before he realized the hour, it was already dark and he fell asleep:

> Thereupon, as he slept, the Christ of God appeared to him with the sign which had appeared in the sky, and urged him to make himself a copy of the sign which had appeared in the sky, and to use this as protection against the attacks of the enemy. [6]

Upon waking, Constantine was apparently still not completely sure what God had instructed him to do, or perhaps he was still awestruck by the power of the vision. He immediately sought out advice from both friends and priests who were travelling with the army. Presumably as Christians, they explained to him the significance of what he had been shown, and that it was a sign that could be used against the forces of evil.

Constantine was now truly convinced by what he had seen, and the interpretations of his Christian friends certainly must have helped him to contextualise this vision, so he summoned goldsmiths and jewellers and instructed them to copy the sign he had seen in gold and precious stones. Of what the goldsmiths and others made, following Constantine's descriptions, Eusebius tells us:

It was constructed to the following design. A tall pole plated with
gold had a transverse bar forming the shape of a cross. Up at the
extreme top a wreath woven of precious stones and gold had been
fastened. On it two letters, intimating by its first characters the
name 'Christ', formed the monogram of the saviour's title, *rho*
being intersected in the middle by *chi*. These letters the Emperor
also used to wear on his helmet in later times. From the transverse
bar, which was bisected by the pole, hung suspended a cloth,
an imperial tapestry covered with a pattern of precious stones
fastened together, which glittered with shafts of light, and inter-
woven with much gold, producing an impression of indescribable
beauty on those who saw it. This banner then, attached to the bar,
was given equal dimensions of length and breadth. But the upright
pole, which extended upwards a long way from its lower end,
below the trophy of the cross and near the top of the tapestry
delineated, carried the golden head-and-shoulders portrait of the
God-beloved Emperor, and likewise of his sons. This saving sign
was always used by the Emperor for protection against every
opposing and hostile force, and he commanded replicas of it to
lead all his armies.[7]

It is surely nothing short of a miracle that such an object could have been
produced so quickly after Constantine's vision; it seems likely that the final
and most beautiful version of the standard was not produced straightaway,
but only much later after many hours of skilled gold-smithing and weaving
had been completed. More importantly, we find out more about what it was
that Constantine himself understood that he had seen in his vision. It would
appear that the 'cross-shaped trophy' was recreated in the gold-plated bars,
though Constantine's standard, from Eusebius' description here, had many
more embellishments that go beyond this simple shape. Although it seems
more likely that Constantine's original vision did not include a vision of
himself and his sons (though these things did end up on the standard) it is
possible to interpret Eusebius as meaning that the *chi rho* (these are the first
two letters of 'Christ' in Greek, which when overlaid make the distinctive
early Christian symbol known as a 'Christogram') were also part of the
original vision, perhaps appearing on the 'cross-shaped trophy' since these
were cast out of gold and jewels, and we are certainly told that it was
goldsmiths and jewellers who had been summoned in particular, and that
they had been given specific descriptions of 'the shape of the sign' and
instructions to recreate this in gold and precious stones.[8]

On the other hand, Constantine's Christian associates could have supplied or suggested this interpretation of the meaning of the 'cross-shaped trophy'; and the Christogram could have been Constantine's attempt to re-imagine his vision as one that was unmistakeably Christian (the Christogram asserting this to be the case) rather than non-specific, as his original vision could perhaps be read as; after all, cross-shapes are not uniquely and undeniably Christian, though granted the cross is an important Christian symbol. Though all this is naturally speculation, Eusebius' wording suggests that once the Christian association had been made, Constantine really took to it and his vision therefore became cemented as a specifically Christian, conversion experience. Eusebius continues:

> They said that the god was the Only begotten Son of the one and only God, and that the sign which appeared was a token of immortality, and was an abiding trophy of the victory over death, which he had once won when he was present on earth. They began to teach him the reasons for his coming, explaining to him in detail the story of his self-accommodation to human conditions. He listened attentively to these accounts too, while he marvelled at the divine manifestation which had been granted to his eyes; comparing the heavenly vision with the meaning of what was being said, he made up his mind, convinced that it was God's own teaching that the knowledge of these things had come to him. He now decided to personally apply himself to the divinely inspired writings. Taking the priests of God as his advisors, he also deemed it right to honour the God who had appeared to him with all due rites. Thereafter, fortified by good hopes in him, he finally set about extinguishing the menacing flames of tyranny.[9]

Notice that the learned Christian men that Constantine had summoned spoke at length on the fundamentals of Christian belief, and that it was after this that Constantine actually and formally became a Christian, since it was this explanation that 'made up his mind'. His conversion was certainly initiated by his intense period of prayer, his vision and subsequent dream, but it was given a context, a framework or a frame of reference by those who were already schooled in the faith.[10]

To those of a sceptic bent, therefore, Constantine's conversion may appear to be not so much sincere but expedient; helpfully fitted into a Christian narrative by those who wanted it to be so (and Constantine himself appears to have wanted this to be the case, given his fervent prayer). Constantine therefore seems to have reasoned that if the Christogram could be used to defeat evil (in the form of Maxentius) then it must be more powerful than the superstitions being employed by his enemy Maxentius, and therefore he was right to switch allegiance to this God.[11] In making this calculation, Constantine seems to have been employing something like the *religio/ superstitio* dichotomy familiar to students of Roman religion.[12]

But to those of a less sceptical bent, another interpretation is just as possible: Constantine did indeed have a vision of a cross and a Christogram, which together do make a distinctive Christian symbol. He quite naturally found this personally meaningful and valid, and so this visionary experience only served to confirm his on-going conversion for him, and perhaps its only significance was therefore to speed it up rather than to actually initiate it. It is entirely possible that even without such a potentially life-changing and significant experience, Constantine would still have converted, especially so if we are to believe Eusebius' report that Constantine was already attracted to Christianity and was already wrestling intellectually with questions of belief. One need not have a vision in order to convert; even without the vision, helpful and powerful though it was, it may well be the case that Constantine had already found enough in Christianity to attract him, and was already sufficiently pro-Christianity from his mother's influence and his upbringing to make his Christian conversion more or less inevitable.

As a final indication of how much personal bias matters when writing history, here is the pagan and anti-Constantine disapproving Zosimus on Constantine's conversion, which as already noted, in the historian's eyes followed on suspiciously closely to his frenzied spate of family murder in 326. Interestingly yet unsurprisingly, in this telling it is Christianity that is associated with effeminacy and suspect orientalism, in the form of an Egyptian ladies' man:

> A certain Egyptian, who had come from Spain to Rome and was intimate with the ladies of the court, met Constantine and assured him that the Christian religion was able to absolve him from guilt and that it promised every wicked man who was converted to it immediate release from all sin. Constantine readily believed what he was told and, abandoning his ancestral religion, embraced the one which the Egyptian offered him.[13]

Whatever the reality of the prayer, the vision, the dream and the subsequent interpretation, the army was definitely reinvigorated on hearing Constantine's welcome news, because Constantine himself was 'fortified by good hopes in him [God], he finally set about extinguishing the menacing flames of tyranny.'[14] And so the army resumed its march south to the deciding battle with the non-Christian Maxentius. Constantine's army marched by way of the *via Flaminia* in mid to late October. Maxentius had marched out of Rome with every man he could muster. It is the subject of much disagreement as to when Maxentius marched north of the Tiber, and whether it was before Constantine arrived on the battlefield; this is not really a crucial point, but I think that the amount of preparation Maxentius made suggests he may have arrived first to allow him to do this.

He crossed the Milvian Bridge and made camp to the north side of the Tiber, only around 2 miles from Rome.[15] Maxentius had been in his camp for several days before Constantine arrived. While Constantine was having his vision and his conversion, neither was Maxentius idle. He had destroyed the Milvian Bridge which had spanned the Tiber in one form or another since the third century BC. This effectively would have trapped his troops on the northern side of a river they could not hope to ford. It also meant that Maxentius' supply lines were severed, except for what could be transported down the Tiber. To prevent his being trapped, he constructed a wooden pontoon bridge across the river. This meant he could escape if necessary, that supplies could be brought in and that the temporary construction could be destroyed, if required, to allow him enough time to get his retreating army to the security of Rome should the coming battle not go well. In the 2-mile plain between the river and Rome, Maxentius also constructed a series of trenches and small fortifications to help cover his retreat if required.

Maxentius deployed his troops very close to the Tiber and with their backs to it. In the Latin Panegyric we are told that they were so close there was no room to regroup if they were to be driven back:

> But how did he arrange his battle line, that little slave who dressed himself in the purple for so many years? Precisely in such a way that no one could escape, that no one driven from his position could withdraw and fight anew, as usually happens, since he would be restrained in front by weapons and in the rear by the river Tiber. In this he did not by Hercules ponder the necessity of resistance but the proximity of refuge, unless perhaps he sensed already that his fatal day had come and wished to drag as many as possible with him as consolation for his own death, to have as companions in his end all who had been partners in his crimes.[16]

Looking past the panegyrical anti-Maxentius rhetoric, it seems that he deployed his men in an unoriginal but traditional formation: three lines of infantry in the centre with cavalry on either wing. However, the other sources for this battle (such as Lactantius, Zosimus and Eusebius) do vary, though this one in particular is the one closest to the events in question. Zosimus relates the events as follows:

> Constantine advanced to Rome with his army and camped before the city in a broad field suitable for a cavalry engagement ... As Maxentius led his army out of Rome and was crossing the bridge that he himself had made, an infinite number of owls flew down and covered the wall. When Constantine saw this, he ordered his men to stand to their arms, and with the armies opposite each other in battle formation, Constantine sent in his horse which attacked and routed the opposing cavalry. As soon as the signal was given to the infantry, they also attacked the enemy in good order. A fierce battle ensued, and although the Romans and the Italian allies shrank from running any risks, hoping to find release from Maxentius' savage tyranny, an immense number of the other soldiers was slain, either trampled by the cavalry or killed by the infantry.[17]

It seems safest to conclude that whatever the precise order of events, Maxentius was the first to set up his troops. Constantine studied his dispositions and deployed his own troops accordingly, essentially as mirroring the enemy formation. The actual battle was a very simple affair in terms of tactics, reading Zosimus closely. Constantine opened the encounter by launching his cavalry on both wings against Maxentius' cavalry. Gallic cavalry were renowned for their quality and they routed the Maxentian cavalry quickly and without difficulty. With the consummate timing indicative of his strategic ability, Constantine ordered forward his infantry against Maxentius' centre at the same time so that their strike coincided with his cavalry wheeling to attack the flanks of Maxentius' infantry.

In the world of Greek and Roman warfare, it was generally the case that heavy infantry could not stand up to an attack from more than one direction simultaneously; this was exactly the preferred tactic of Alexander the Great and worked brilliantly for him every time. However, if there were any troops in the Roman world able to react to this, it would have to be the disciplined Roman legionaries. Their short swords, inbuilt flexibility and training in adaptability meant that they could turn to face a new enemy with relative ease. Having said this, morale mattered a great deal also: the Italian infantry under Maxentius seemingly did not have any great desire either to fight for Maxentius, or indeed against Constantine, and they didn't put up much of a fight so they were quickly driven back.

The battle in the very centre was the fiercest; the Praetorian Guard performed their designated duty of defending the Emperor admirably and they fought hard to protect Maxentius. But ultimately this was to no avail. The Maxentian infantry quickly gave ground, but as already noted, they were stationed so close to the river that there was little ground to give. Instead, they broke and tried to flee across the wooden bridge. Being a temporary structure, however, it was not built to take the weight of thousands of armoured infantry running across in a panicked stampede. The pontoon bridge broke apart while many Romans were fleeing across it, including Maxentius himself; given the weight of their armour and the depth of the river, those who fell from the bridge had little chance and many drowned, including Maxentius. His body was later recovered by Constantine, beheaded, and his head placed atop a spear as Constantine marched on Rome. Zosimus records his death:

> As long as his cavalry stood firm, Maxentius seemed to have some hope, but when they gave way, he fled with the rest across the bridge to the city. The timbers, unable to carry the weight, broke and Maxentius himself with a great many others was swept away down stream.[18]

This cruel yet triumphal act reminds us that regardless of the new ideas Constantine had just taken onboard, these were still essentially filtered through his personality and his status as a military man vying for control of the Roman Empire. The main justification for this brutal act of power and humiliation was for Constantine to clearly demonstrate to the people of Rome that the hated usurper was dead and they were now free of his tyranny. This myth-making worked very well: Constantine was welcomed by the populace as the liberator he was so desperate to be. Zosimus on this:

> When news of this victory reached the city, no one dared rejoice at what had happened, because some thought the report was false, but when Maxentius' head was brought in on a spear, they abandoned fear and their dejection turned to joy. Since this was the outcome of events, Constantine punished only a few of Maxentius' closest associates, but he disbanded the Praetorian Guard and destroyed the forts where it was quartered. After settling affairs in Rome, he set out for Gaul.[19]

He had defeated barbarians, defended the empire and protected the citizens of Rome; he had ticked all the boxes on the list of what every good Roman emperor should do, though note how Constantine's major destructive act upon entering Rome was to disband the Praetorian Guard because they had been loyal to Maxentius (this being manifestly unfair; this was, after all, the reason the Guard had been instituted in the first place and their remit was to protect the person of the emperor, even if he were unpopular). Though Constantine did allow defeated soldiers and Praetorians to take up service within his army, those who accepted this offer were sent to the Rhine frontier; no doubt to replace troops loyal to him that he had to take from that area to reinforce his field command.

Had Maxentius committed a sin of omission by leaving the security of Rome's fortifications? Perhaps not; his reasons for doing so are at least understandable. Romans believed in omens with conviction, and he should not be criticised too harshly for that. The lack of trust he placed in the Roman populace, and the likelihood of betrayal is a stronger strategic motivation (and we do know he was unpopular) and in many ways a sound one given the size of his force being at least equal to that of Constantine. Maxentius' major strategic mistake was threefold:

- Fighting on the north side of the Tiber.
- Placing his back to the river.
- Destroying the Milvian Bridge and allowing himself no good means of escape when his plans backfired, other than over a rickety and makeshift wooden bridge which was not equal to the task.

This trinity of strategic mistakes worked to give him a quick and decisive defeat, as well as costing him his own life in the process. Of course, with the benefit of hindsight it is difficult to imagine why Maxentius made any of these mistakes, let alone all three together. He was a fatally-flawed poor commander, as evidenced here by his bad strategy and by his lack of desire to command the northern forces at Verona, preferring the safety of Rome. For his own career it was a pity he did not have an Agrippa, but he did not and paid the price with his life, and Constantine became the emperor in Rome. With his victory at the Milvian Bridge, Constantine had made himself sole ruler in the west. His empire was large, wealthy and powerful, but his ambition did not stop there. Half of the empire still lay outside of his control.

Chapter 6

Campus Ergenus

Just one day after victory at the Milvian Bridge, Constantine entered Rome with the head of Maxentius on a lance at the vanguard of the army. Eusebius speaks in glowing terms of the emperor's reception from the populace of Rome:

> Immediately all the members of the senate and other persons there of fame and distinction, as if released from a cage, and all the peoples of Rome, gave him a bright-eyed welcome with spontaneous acclamations and unbounded joy. Men with their wives and children and countless numbers of slaves with unrestrained cheers pronounced him their redeemer, saviour and benefactor.[1]

Eusebius' choice of language is illustrative of how he wished Constantine and Maxentius to be seen. He twice uses language that suggests that the conqueror was freeing Rome and its citizens from whatever horrors Maxentius had visited upon them. The deliberate intention of this rhetoric was to portray Constantine as liberator of the Romans and nothing like a foreign conqueror from Gaul. For his part, Constantine appears to have accepted the acclamation of the crowds with humility. Eusebius goes on:

> He, however, being possessed of inward fear of God, was not inflated by the cries nor over-exuberance at their praises, but was conscious of the help of God; so he immediately offered up a prayer of thanksgiving to the giver of his victory.[2]

This act of prayer would have been the first obvious hint to the Roman people of the religious changes that Constantine's victory would bring. Constantine's victory parade wound through the streets of Rome, and naturally the emperor would have wanted to ensure as many people as possible had the opportunity to see their liberator. This spectacle, we can speculate, would have felt something like a successful football team returning on an open top bus with some trophy on display; only in this case the trophy was the head of Maxentius.

Despite the slow approach to the Forum, probably there were those who still felt Constantine's victory parade was proceeding too rapidly for them to get a good look at the Emperor. We often forget in this modern age of mass communication that ordinary citizens would almost never have had the opportunity to actually see their rulers. Their main view of their rulers would likely come from representations on coins, and we can only imagine the press, rush and excitement of the crowds as everyone jostled to get to the front and look.

This procession would not only have acted to glorify and advertise the new Emperor, but also his conversion. The crowds would have seen the new standard towards the head of the army with the Christogram on it. Those nearest to the front also could not have failed to see the same design painted on the shields of the troops: among the crowds, one wonders how widely familiar and understood this symbol would have been.

Moreover, Constantine did not just wear his new religious belief; he enacted it. New Emperors typically approached the Capitoline Hill and made sacrifices in the temples there in thanksgiving, but Constantine did not do this. He essentially rejected Jupiter in favour of entering the imperial palace and praying to his new God. This public display can hardly have been missed or ignored by the watching hordes, but just in case they had, Constantine would soon leave nobody in any doubt of his new religious leanings.

Constantine did not immediately follow up his victory at the Milvian Bridge by attempting to conquer any more of the Empire; for the meantime he chose to stay in Rome and consolidate his position. As part of this consolidation process he initiated a massive building programme. First of all, he ordered the completion of a project started by Maxentius, a massive new courthouse called the Basilica Nova.[3] This was located in the Forum and was to be one of the largest buildings in Rome. This is the building which housed the colossal statue of the emperor, showing him both pointing and looking up towards heaven. The inscription at the base of the statue read:

> By this salutary sign, the true proof of valour, I liberated your city, saved from the tyrant's yoke; moreover the Senate and People of Rome I liberated and restored to their ancient splendour and brilliance.[4]

Along with the building programme, Constantine took a number of religious leaders into his inner circle and consulted them on policy matters, which is how he spent the remainder of 312. He also used his break in Rome to study the scriptures of his new religion.[5] As a reward for his victories he was awarded the title 'Senior Augustus' by the Senate, legitimising his rule over the western empire; but while he was consolidating and cementing his position in Rome, he was also communicating with his eastern colleagues. He sent an edict to both Licinius and Maximin declaring toleration for Christians; prior to this Maximin in particular had engaged in episodes of persecution.

He also sought to strengthen his existing political alliance with Licinius, his closest neighbour and the man who, though not actively supporting him against Maxentius, had not actually interfered. Constantine offered Licinius the hand of his sister, Constantia, to strengthen their alliance. In order that Maximin did not feel entirely left out, he had the Senate declare Constantine and Maximin joint consuls for the year 313.

Constantine left Rome in mid-to-late January 313, heading for a pre-arranged meeting with Licinius in Milan. The journey was short and uneventful with the two meeting at the beginning of February. This was something of a summit meeting for the two leading figures, and expectations were probably high. Licinius agreed to issue an edict in the parts of the empire that he controlled ordering toleration of the Christians. He also recognized Constantine as senior Augustus in the western empire. In return, Licinius was granted the right to make laws in his parts of the empire as well as accepting the hand of Constantia.[6] To celebrate the occasion, coins were minted depicting both emperors together in a move designed to indicate their accord to the citizenry.[7]

This initial agreement was just the first part of the story. The two men evidently discussed military issues including the defence of the frontiers, but by far the bulk of the conversation was on religious matters. Licinius had been conducting a policy of toleration of the Christians since the edict of Galerius in 311. Simple toleration though was never going to be enough to satisfy Constantine's new religious beliefs and his desire to advance the cause, and he pushed Licinius for far more.

Beyond toleration, Constantine wanted full and open acceptance of Christianity, an end to all persecution, the return of property that had been appropriated and full legal rights and protection for Christians. From Constantine's perspective he was lucky to be negotiating with a man who was at least tolerant of Christianity and Christians. For Licinius, he needed Constantine as a key ally in order that he could continue his hostilities with Maximin without the fear of having to fight on two fronts.

Licinius agreed to Constantine's demands for his own political reasons. He did not have the same religious sentiment as the western emperor (after all, unlike Constantine he hadn't fought a crucial battle in which he thought that decisive divine support was given to him from this God), but was keen to deal with Maximin and this agreement would help him to that goal. The formal agreement that came out of this meeting was, it is fair to say, one of the most important ever produced in the history of the Roman Empire. The 'Edict of Milan' was issued jointly and in essence declared the Roman Empire to be Christian, at least in name. Before the edict could be fully implemented in the east, Licinius first had to remove Maximin from power.

With Constantine thoroughly ensconced in the west, and Licinius' western and southern borders secure after the extended treaty with Constantine, there was little doubt that war between Maximin and Licinius was imminent. Maximin had not been best pleased at the Senate's decision to declare Constantine the senior Augustus, and had further been alarmed by the marriage of Licinius to Constantia and the closer political alliance that that event boded forth. He was also not fooled by the sop Constantine offered of the joint consulship for 313. Maximin would likely have seen no alternative to war with Licinius, and the Edict of Milan was simply the final straw. Maximin was not a Christian, and he had been vigorously persecuting members of that religion for some time; he was in no mood to stop on the say-so of somebody he would have seen as the usurping senior emperor.[8]

With war now inevitable, Maximin decided to strike first in the hope of defeating Licinius before he was fully prepared to offer resistance. Maximin evidently had a substantial field army that he gathered together and set off across Anatolia towards the Bosporus. Despite suffering terrible losses in his baggage train, largely due to the poor winter weather, once at the Bosporus he crossed, entering Licinian territory, and immediately attacked Byzantium. The city was bravely defended by a small garrison loyal to Licinius; it resisted bribery and assault for eleven days, but could hold out no longer than this and surrendered.[9] Maximin then captured Heraclea and continued to drive Licinius' forces westwards.

Licinius was unaware of the threat until Maximin was at the walls of Byzantium, and it took him a little time to react. He gathered together his mobile field army and marched east to meet the invader. By the time he moved, however, Maximin was well into Thrace, capturing cities as he went. To counter this, Licinius' field army was not large; he suffered the same difficulties as Constantine had against Maxentius in that he was in control of one of the most difficult border regions of the empire. Licinius could not denude the Danube frontier of troops to aid his resistance to Maximin as this would have left the region defenceless against barbarians from the lands north of the empire. As a result, Licinius was able to command only around 30,000 men. Opposed to him were 70,000 men under Maximin.

At around the time Maximin captured Heraclea, Licinius was close to Adrianople, around 29km from Heraclea.[10] Licinius' scouts would have told him of the location of Maximin's forces, so he looked for a suitable battle-field close to Adrianople. He decided upon the *Campus Ergenus* between Adrianople and Heraclea, set up his army there and waited for the coming battle.[11] Lactantius tells us that, on the eve of the battle, Licinius received a visitation in a dream from an angel and dictated the wording of the prayer to be given to his men before the battle. The story is, needless to say, suspiciously similar to Constantine's experiences before the Milvian Bridge, and it seems a little more likely that the idea for this event and the prayer itself were given to Licinius by Constantine prior to his leaving Milan.[12]

Having received the prayer, Licinius' army waited for the approach of Maximin. Licinius was hoping that the battle would be fought on 1 May, the anniversary of Maximin's accession. This would have been a fitting parallel to Maxentius' final battle. Maximin had other ideas, however, and made haste to the battlefield, arriving on 30 April.[13] As the two armies stood opposed to each other, Licinius gave an order that is perhaps unique in the ancient world: he ordered his men to lay down their arms, shields and helmets. Upon doing this they recited the prayer that Licinius had given them, three times, in unison.[14]

The two commanders seemingly wished to come to an amicable solution, despite there being the small matter of close to 100,000 men standing on the plain ready for battle. They attempted a negotiated settlement; we do not know what was demanded by each commander, but in the end neither party could agree. Maximin seems to have believed that the religious differences between the two commanders was a key factor and he made offers to Licinius' troops to go over to his side; he evidently believed that they were simply obeying orders from above when they simultaneously recited their prayer. But Licinius' men stood firm in their new faith.

Battle commenced. Maximin set his men up in a rigid defensive formation, allowing Licinius to take the lead. It is rare, but not unheard of, for an army outnumbered by more than 2:1 to be the aggressor; but that is apparently what Maximin's defensive strategy resulted in. We do not know enough about the battle to be able to reconstruct it properly, but it seems that Maximin's men initially had the upper hand, but as the fighting wore on, Licinius' Illyrian troops gradually came good and drove Maximin's men back.[15]

When defeat seemed inevitable, Maximin apparently changed clothes in order to slip away unnoticed. He and the remainder of his defeated army fled the field and made straight for the Bosporus and the relative safety of Asia Minor: territory he controlled. Despite his rapid flight, Licinius pursued him relentlessly. Once across the Bosporus, Maximin passed through Nicomedia on 2 May, only pausing long enough to collect his family before resuming his flight eastwards into the interior of Asia Minor. At some point during his flight he again assumed the purple robes of the emperor and, at the head of the tattered remains of his army, made for the Cilician Gates to once again offer battle to Licinius' pursuing forces.

Licinius was again relentless in his pursuit and this time Maximin had had no respite from his constant forced marches. Maximin's attempt at organized resistance at the Cilician Gates crumbled as soon as Licinius began his assault, and once again Maximin was forced to flee. Maximin reached Tarsus, which he believed to be a city with strong enough defences to resist a siege if required. Licinius arrived shortly afterwards and almost immediately began to invest the city. He did not possess a siege train, he had been moving too rapidly for any such cumbersome equipment to be allowed to slow him down. His only option was scaling ladders and battering rams, handily each of which could be manufactured locally at short notice.

From Licinius' perspective, the siege was prosecuted vigorously and it was only a matter of time before his Illyrians broke through the city's defences. The situation was also obvious to Maximin; he had no means of escape and had no wish to be captured alive by Licinius' forces. His only option was suicide in such a situation, which he took in the high summer of 313.[16] This left only Constantine and Licinius in positions of power; Constantine controlling the western empire, Licinius controlling the empire in the east.

This collection of marble fragments, now on display in the Capitoline Museums in Rome, is all that remains from a huge statue of Constantine.

This close-up view of the head from the same collection depicts Constantine's eyes as if raised towards God in prayer or supplication.

A bronze head of Constantine on display in the Capitoline Museum in Rome.

ISTANTINE BY THIS SIGN CONQUER

This bronze statue of Constantine can be found outside the entrance to the South Transept of York Minster, and was erected in 1998. It commemorates the proclamation of Constantine as emperor by his troops at Eboracum in 306. In fact, the remains of a Roman fortress can be found beneath York Minster itself, and it is therefore likely that this ceremony took place not that far from the site of the modern-day statue.

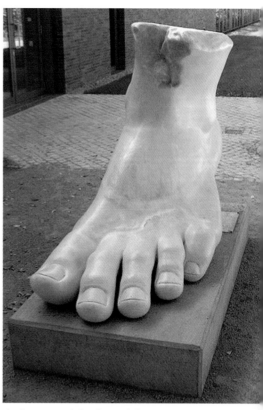

A marble bust of Constantine dating from the fourth century AD, on display in the Vatican Museums, Rome.

A close-up of the foot of this same statue, giving an idea of how immense the complete version must have been.

This fresco shows the Baptism of Constantine by students of Raphael and is dated to 1520–1524. It can be found in the Sala di Constantino, on the west wall.

This oil on panel painting by Rubens, *The Emblem of Christ Appearing to Constantine*, dated to 1622, is in fact a preparatory sketch for a series of tapestries showing Constantine's life. It is now in the Philadelphia Museum of Art.

This fresco (the section here reproduced in black and white) shows the Battle of the Milvian Bridge, by students of Raphael (Giulio Romano, Francesco Penni and Raffaellino del Colle) and is dated to 1520–1524. It adorns the Sala di Constantino, one of 'Raphael's Rooms' in the Vatican, along with frescos showing the Vision of the Cross, the Baptism of Constantine and the so-called Donation of Constantine. Together they demonstrate the after-life of Constantine's life and career, and how interlinked his Christian conversion was with his military victory and secular power in the visual culture and imagination of the church.

Hagia Sophia in modern-day Istanbul is possibly the most famous building associated with Constantine's conversion. Although the first church was not dedicated until 360, legend has it that the edifice was built by Constantine and was one of the most impressive ecclesiastical buildings yet seen. After its collapse, and two subsequent rebuilds, the emperor Justinian decided to build a third church, that would be one of the wonders of the world, in 532. This is the building which is still famed today, in particular for its massive dome.

The ramparts of Istanbul. Constantine started fortifying Constantinople in 324 with a single wall, which was completed by his son Constantius II. However, the exact location of this wall is not now known and the city had already grown beyond its confines by as early as the fifth century. During the Byzantine period it was replaced as the main defence by the Theodosian Walls which enclosed a wider area. These in turn have been rebuilt many times over the years and sections of them are shown here as they have currently been restored.

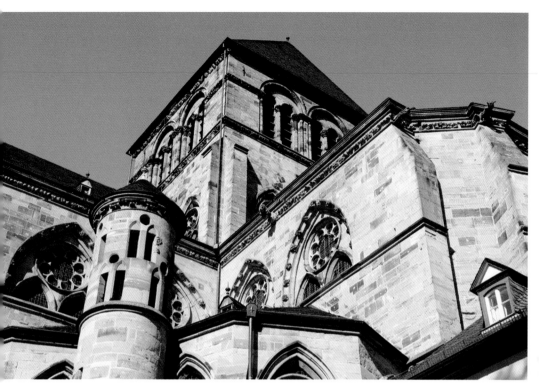

This photograph shows the oldest church in Germany, the Trier Cathedral, Dom St Peter. As part of Constantine's ambitious religious building programme, the Bishop Maximin of Trier managed the construction of some of the greatest western churches outside Rome. The Constantinian church covered an area four times the size of the present cathedral, and was replete with four basilicas and a baptistery. However, the church of the fourth century was destroyed by the Franks and later rebuilt; not the first time in its history.

The life and works of Constantine have captured the imagination of great painters throughout history. For example, Canaletto's painting, The Arch of Constantine (1742) which is currently housed in the Royal Collection. The view of the Arch of Constantine is from the south: the side of the Colosseum can just be seen the right, as can be the church of San Pietro through the centre which makes this clear.

A gold multiple minted in Ticinum in 313. It shows Constantine victorious in the foreground and *Sol Invictus* in the background. Currently housed in the Cabinet des Médailles in the Bibliotèque nationale de France in Paris.

A gold multiple minted in Nicomedia in 320, showing Licinius' father and son. Currently housed in the Cabinet des Médailles in the Bibliotèque nationale de France in Paris.

This photograph shows the Rotunda in Thessaloniki, Greece. The round building was built in 306 by Galerius, to be his mausoleum. It was later converted into a church by Constantine, an example of how older existing buildings were taken over or adapted for Christian usage after his conversion. A minaret is visible in this picture, reminding us that this process of adaption and conversion is hardly restricted to Christianity: once the city of Thessaloniki fell to the Ottoman Turks in 1590 the church was converted to a mosque.

Chapter 7

War with Licinius: The Battle of Cibalae and Campus Ardiensis

While Licinius was engaged with Maximin, Constantine stayed in Italy, largely to see who would be victorious in their eastern civil war. Despite Licinius' alliance with Constantine, the western Emperor appears to have offered little in the way of actual help to his ally, but Licinius had only needed the assurance that his western and southern border was secure so as to allow him to pour all of his energies into the east.

Once Licinius was victorious and began chasing Maximin eastwards into Asia Minor, Constantine realised that he had backed the winning side and began campaigning again himself. Constantine's first movement was back into Gaul to suppress a small band of Franks who had crossed the Rhine frontier.[1] Constantine's return to Gaul was in the late spring of 313; likely at the head of only a portion of the field army. We can assume this because the Frankish raid was small and did not trouble Constantine military-wise. Once victory had been achieved he returned to Trier to refresh his troops. The Frankish incursion was either small bands crossing the frontier who really were looking for plunder, or else it was a feint to draw Constantine away from northern Italy. The hand of probability comes down on the former explanation as the latter would imply a level of co-operation amongst the Franks that we cannot prove.

While Constantine was in Gaul, a larger band of Franks began massing for what would have been a large-scale invasion of northern Italy. Upon realising the danger to Italy, Constantine made a series of forced marches back across the Alps and the threat faded away without materialising in an actual invasion.

This tit-for-tat is an excellent microcosm of the wider situation on the Rhine and Danube borders. If the status quo obtained, then neither side was strong enough to defeat the other. If the Romans weakened their border forces, then the barbarians would readily invade and would quickly defeat the border forces. If an emperor strengthened one sector in order to cross the frontier, then another sector would almost certainly have to be weakened to allow this and the barbarians would look to exploit that. The border situation was approaching a stalemate, despite the might of the Roman Empire behind one side, but Constantine wanted to try and tip the balance far more in his own favour.

Constantine understood the complex military situation on the frontier better than most, and he was a good enough commander to formulate a strategy for defeating the Franks that was rather more complex and subtle than simply crossing the Rhine in outright force. Constantine's cunning strategy was to lure the enemy across the Rhine into territory of his choosing and defeat them in Roman-controlled lands. In order to achieve this he marched in the direction of southern Germany with a large army, feigning an intention to campaign in that region. The Franks quickly massed on the newly-denuded sections of the frontier and crossed the Rhine into Roman territory, believing it to be largely undefended.

While he moved south with the majority of the army, he had left pockets of troops to oppose any such crossing by the Franks. Once the Franks started to cross in numbers, these Romans emerged from their concealment (presumably quietly stepping out from behind small copses of trees) and began to engage the enemy. The Franks would not have been worried by a much smaller Roman force, and continued to cross the Rhine. Once the majority were across and the battle was at its zenith, Constantine made a surprise return at the head of a fleet sailing up the Rhine. This naval force trapped the Franks in a classic pincer and also cut off their escape route to safety across the Rhine.

The Franks were outmanoeuvred and in an impossible position. Many did manage to escape back across the Rhine, but they were pursued by Constantine who knew he had the opportunity to deliver a crushing blow to that particular tribe. There is source evidence to suggest that Constantine won victories over the Franks in the summer of 313; he heartily prosecuted his offensive across the Rhine, burning towns and settlements and slaughtering many civilians. The result was certainly the pacification of the region for several years, and the events are recorded by the Panegyricist, though with the usual excess to be expected of the genre:

> Worn out by battles and sated with victories you did not, as Nature demands, give yourself up to leisure and rest, but on the same march on which you returned to your Gauls you continued to the border of Lower Germany. Of course, after such a great

interval of time and such a short distance between locations – after a campaign of a year's duration – you immediately began operations from the Tiber to the Rhine, or rather (as the omen and similarity of names as well as your greatness of spirit, Emperor, promise) you will extend the Empire from Tuscan Albula [the River Tiber] to German Alba [the River Albis, modern Elbe: the geography is unlikely] . . . You alone, Constantine, tirelessly follow one war with another, heap one victory upon another. As if the past is blotted out if you cease, you think you have not conquered unless you are conquering.[2]

In late summer, Constantine returned victorious to Trier. He was now in a very strong position both militarily and politically. The frontier was secure for the first time in decades, he was sole ruler in the west and he had a strong alliance with Licinius who was now the sole ruler in the east. Constantine would undoubtedly have felt that he had a lot for which to thank his new patron deity, and his military success undoubtedly also reinforced and strengthened his conversion experience. Constantine appears to have spent the next two years in relative peace and security, spending many months in Trier and some time in Rome; but by the autumn of 316, war with Licinius seemed inevitable.

In 315/6 when Constantine was likely preparing for war, Licinius had not been idle. He had campaigned extensively on the Persian frontier in an attempt to secure that region. He had then returned to mainland Europe where he conducted an extensive campaign against the Goths of the Danube region. By the summer of 316 he had returned to Sirmium in Pannonia where he set up something of a temporary capital in the western reaches of his domain.[3]

The war was most likely of Constantine's making, but given its decisive nature, this needs further examination. Constantine sent Constantius as an emissary to Licinius carrying a proposal to create another Caesar. This would have been a man called Bassianus and the proposal was that Italy would be his territory, and one must suspect that he would also have proposed a second Caesar to restore the Tetrarchy, but there is little evidence for this speculation.[4]

Licinius rejected the proposal and, apparently, persuaded Bassianus (through his brother, Senecio) into an assassination attempt on Constantine. The attempt failed completely and Senecio fled to Licinius' protection in the east. Constantine demanded he be handed over for trial, but Licinius refused. War was the inevitable outcome. The dates of the events leading to the war are not certain, but we do know that Constantine marched into Licinian territory without much delay (he must have been preparing for the war for some time) and the Battle of Cibalae was fought between the two Augusti on 8 October 316. Zosimus records the lead up to hostilities:

> The empire thus devolved on Constantine and Licinius and in a very short while they fell out with each other. Licinius did not give the occasion for it; rather Constantine, as was his way, broke faith over agreements made with him, and tried to detach one of the provinces which belonged to Licinius' empire. Thus their enmity was brought into the open and both gathered armies and met for battle. Licinius established his headquarters at Cibalis, a hillside city in Pannonia. The road leading to it is narrow, with a deep marsh (some five stades wide) lying alongside a great part of it and the rest mountainous, including the hill on which the city stands. Below it is a spacious plain, boundless to behold. Here Licinius encamped, spreading his battle line right up to the hill, to protect his wings.[5]

In comparison, Eusebius is in no doubt that this was a kind of holy war. He tells us that Constantine: 'reckoned that it must be a pious and holy act by removing one man to rescue most of the human race'.[6] Whether Constantine saw it in exactly those terms is debatable, but there is surely no real reason to doubt that he had some measure of a religious take on the civil war with Licinius.

Before the war began, Licinius gathered together a select group of his bodyguards and the senior commanders who would accompany him on the campaign. They met in a sacred grove where there were various images of what Licinius 'thought were gods [which] were erected in it, carved in stone', the emperor then 'lit candles to them, and made the usual sacrifices'.[7] After this typically pagan ceremony, Licinius addressed the assembled men:

> Friends and comrades, these are our ancestral gods, whom we honour because we have received them for worship from our earliest forefathers. The commander of those arrayed against us has broken faith with the ancestral code and adopted godless belief, mistakenly acknowledging some foreign god from somewhere or other, and he even shames his own army with this god's disgraceful emblem. Now is the moment which will prove which one is mistaken in his belief: it will decide between the gods honoured by us and by the other party. Either it will declare us victors, and so quite rightly demonstrate that our gods are true saviours and helpers, or else, if this one god of Constantine's whoever he

is and wherever he sprang from, defeats our troops who are very numerous, who are very numerous and perhaps numerically superior, let no one hereafter be in doubt which god he ought to worship, since he should go over to the winner and offer him the prizes of victory. If the foreign god, whom we now mock should prove superior, let nothing stop us from acknowledging and honouring him too, saying goodbye to these, whose candles we light in vain. But if ours prevail, which is not in doubt, after our victory here let us launch the war against the godless.[8]

According to Eusebius, in another parallel of a kind to Constantine's vision before the Milvian Bridge, those present had their own vision. They apparently saw in the sky an image of Constantine's forces marching into the cities of the east: a sure portent of things to come.

Constantine's army was relatively small, being only 20,000 in number. This would have been a large proportion of his mobile field army. He could not risk taking more because the Rhine and Danube frontiers still had to be defended, and a strategic reserve needed to be left in case of a barbarian incursion that successfully penetrated the troops of the *limitanei*. Licinius, on the other hand, outnumbered Constantine by almost 2:1, commanding 35,000 troops. Licinius was well inside his own borders so could bring much of his field army to bear, although by no means all of the troops he had at his disposal. This fact alone suggests that Licinius was not entirely expecting such an aggressive move, or more likely he was not expecting it quite so soon.

Constantine's relatively small force could march quickly along the roads of the eastern Roman Empire, and the route he chose was particularly conducive to this; Cibalae being on the main road to the major city of Sirmium, a city in Pannonia, on one side of which runs the River Savus, which flows into the Danube. When Constantine reached the field of battle, he surveyed the terrain as well as the relative size and dispositions of the two opposing forces. We know little of the actual events of the battle save for a few details, as Zosimus relates:

> Constantine marshalled his army near the mountain; he thought it was an advantage to have the horse in front, lest the enemy should fall on the infantry which moved up more slowly and prevent its advance owing to the difficulty of the ground. Thereupon, being the master of swift attack, he raised the signal and straightaway charged the enemy. The battle that followed was almost the fiercest ever, for when each side had fired their arrows, they engaged for a long time with spears and javelins. It began in the morning and lasted till night, when the right wing, where Constantine

was, prevailed and his opponents turned to flight. When Licinius'
troops saw him mounting his horse and ready for flight, they no
longer held their ground or took their supper, but abandoned their
cattle, pack-animals and all other equipment and, carrying with
them food to satisfy their hunger for only that night, marched
with all speed with Licinius to Sirmium. As he passed this town,
he broke down the bridge over the river, before proceeding with
the intention of raising an army in the countries around Thrace.[9]

So as we know from this source, the battle started quite early in the day
(presumably after a tense night of each side watching for signs of a night
attack) and neither side likely getting much rest. The fighting was initially
slow to develop, but lasted for most of the day. Both sides were content to
begin hostilities from a distance by using their missile troops to try and break
the lines of their respective enemies, but with little success; missile troops
seldom had a great effect against the heavily armoured legions. The close-
quarters fighting began perhaps late morning, and this lasted for much
of the rest of the day. The fighting was fierce as each side knew full well
the potential consequences of defeat. The cavalry appeared to have been
an important factor in the Battle of Cibalae, since they were tasked with
ensuring that the infantry were protected in making their slower advance
over rough terrain:

> Constantine marshalled his army near the mountain; he thought it
> was an advantage to have the horse in front, lest the enemy should
> fall on the infantry which moved up more slowly and prevent
> its advance owing to the difficulty of the ground. Thereupon,
> being master of the swift attack, he raised the signal and straight-
> away charged the enemy. The battle that followed was almost the
> fiercest ever, for when each side had fired their arrows, they engaged
> for a long time with spears and javelins. It began in the morning
> and lasted till night, when the right wing, where Constantine was,
> prevailed and his opponents turned to flight.'[10]

Licinius made his escape under cover of darkness and made for his base at
Sirmium where he had left behind his family and part of his treasury.[11] The
heaviest losses in any ancient battle would have occurred to Licinius' troops
at this point, with some estimating 20,000 dead. These losses are likely
exaggerated, however, as they probably were in almost every ancient battle.

Licinius did not delay in Sirmium for long, and after the briefest of
delays he left Sirmium and headed southeast towards and then into Thrace.
For Licinius at least, there seems little belief that he could negotiate an easy

peace after his decisive defeat or perhaps just as likely, little willingness on his part to come to terms with the western emperor whom he saw as the aggressor in this new conflict. For Licinius, decisive action was required. During his retreat, Licinius raised Valens to the status of Augustus. This was an act that was guaranteed to insult Constantine. At the time of his elevation, Valens was a minor commander of one of Licinius' border regions, but he had evidently proved himself a capable commander, and Licinius needed such men. Valens was also evidently quite influential in his own region as he quickly raised a substantial army close to Adrianople.

Whilst heading into Thrace, Licinius had attempted to buy himself more time by destroying the bridge over the River Savus at Singidunum. After his victory, Constantine did not sit on his laurels, but gave chase to his fleeing eastern counterpart. Constantine was advancing with at least the majority of his army and could not move quite as quickly as Licinius who would have likely only had the remnants of his army in attendance. For Constantine, this was not a headlong pursuit like that of Alexander the Great chasing Darius after the latter's defeat at the Battle of Gaugamela in 331. Constantine was probably a more cautious character than the lucky Macedonian tactical genius, and no doubt believed that he would catch Licinius either way at some point.

Constantine was not moving fast enough to stop Licinius destroying the vital bridge, so when he arrived at the River Savus his men had to rebuild it, delaying them for several days at least. This allowed Licinius enough time to join up the remnants of his existing force with the new army that had been raised quickly by Valens to form a new and very substantial army to oppose Constantine. It seems unlikely that Valens could have raised an entirely new army in such a limited time; more likely Licinius was getting desperate, and this was the remains of his field army along with many troops being stripped from the frontier. If Licinius lost, then what did it matter if the barbarians from the region gave Constantine problems? And if he won, then he could deal with the potential new threat at his leisure.

When Constantine reached the Thracian city of Philippi, Licinius evidently decided to try another attempt at diplomacy, given that he believed that he was again in a strong bargaining position, being at the head of a large army on terrain he knew well (he had defeated Maximin in this area only three years previously).[12] Constantine received the embassy from Licinius, and at first glance was not fundamentally opposed to the idea. Constantine sent a counter proposal back to Licinius that he would make peace if the latter dismissed the lowly Valens from his newly elevated position.[13]

Constantine in all probability would not have expected Licinius to cede to these demands, but possibly with an eye to his image, he did not want to be seen as the aggressor, or perhaps wanted to buy some time of his own to reform his army after their, albeit leisurely, pursuit. Licinius simply could not accept Constantine's proposal because if he dismissed Valens, then Valens' army may well follow. The new army were very much Valens' men after all, and were men he had commanded for a period of time on the frontier and so would have felt some personal loyalty towards him.

Now with that, a second encounter was inevitable. The battle took place between Adrianople and Philippi at a place called *Campus Ardiensis* in January of 317.[14] We know even less about the course of this battle than about its predecessor several weeks previously. We do know that again it began early in the day; again it was a very lengthy affair with neither side able to deliver a decisive blow at any point down the line. The battle also lasted until late and it was when the sun was beginning to set that Licinius finally admitted defeat and fled under cover of darkness again.[15]

Eusebius preserves a very interesting titbit of information on Constantine and his conduct of the battle, something that we can reasonably assume the western emperor continued into future battles. He tells us that Constantine's victory was in large part because of the trophy that his army carried into battle:

> Where this was displayed, there ensued a rout of the enemy, and pursuit by the victors. The emperor became aware of this, and wherever he saw a unit of his own army in difficulties, he would give orders for the saving trophy to give support there as a sort of victorious antidote. Victory would at once ensue, as courage and strength by some divine favour braced up the strugglers.[16]

After seeing the impact upon morale of this trophy, and the victory that came in every sector where it appeared, Constantine made some organisational changes within the army to ensure this could continue to happen, without the risk of the trophy falling into Licinius' hands. Constantine ordered some of his own bodyguard to form into a separate unit to carry and protect the trophy. These were men of particular martial distinction and piety, numbering fifty. Their assigned task was to carry the trophy, each man taking turns, into the thick of the battle in order to give a boost to the Constantinian troops in that sector.

Despite the effects of the trophy, real or otherwise, the battle was hard fought, but eventually defeat came to Licinius, who again managed to evade Constantine's grasp. Having gained this second victory over Licinius, Constantine may have reasonably expected resistance to collapse, at least in Europe, but he was mistaken: Licinius was not beaten yet.

Licinius was not so lowly. He was an able field commander with a wealth of experience on the eastern front, and indeed against Roman opposition during his rise to the status of eastern emperor. Constantine quite reasonably expected his enemy to retreat towards Byzantium and perhaps further into his own territory, but Licinius had other ideas. Anticipating that Constantine would expect this, and fearing that he may encounter an advance guard of Constantine before he reached safety, Licinius and Valens both decided to move north towards Beroea instead of east towards Byzantium.[17]

In an excellent object lesson in the reality of the quality of military intelligence in the ancient world, Constantine quickly advanced eastwards towards Byzantium and as he thought, towards another expected encounter with his adversary. Once Constantine had headed east with the majority of his army, Licinius and Valens with the remnants of their defeated army headed back south once more, with the goal of severing the lines of supply and communication to Constantine's army.

By this very simple stratagem, Licinius was again able to put himself in a strong negotiating position. Licinius, this time apparently more robustly and with some hope of success, sued for peace with Constantine. The latter was amenable to the discussions, largely because of his difficult position, and so serious peace negotiations began. These lasted some time as a treaty was not signed for another couple of months, on 1 March 317. Constantine's main stipulations were: firstly he was to be ceded all lands in Europe with the exception of Thrace, Moesia and Scythia Minor (these were to remain under the control of Licinius). Secondly, Valens was to be removed from his position. Licinius, having been defeated twice in battle by Constantine, felt he had little choice but to agree to these seemingly reasonable demands. Valens was removed from his position and Licinius even went to the extent of having him executed shortly afterwards as a reward for his service.[18] Two new Caesars were also crowned as part of the settlement.

The treaty was finally ratified on 1 March 317 at Serdica. In many ways, we must consider Licinius to have received quite a generous deal from Constantine. Licinius, after all, had been twice defeated by a numerically inferior army as commanded by Constantine. The western emperor could easily have either demanded more territory or else continued the campaign eastwards to finally defeat Licinius, no doubt with the price being his life. Constantine likely either felt unsure of his military strength or else did not want to remove a significant number of troops from the border regions of the Rhine and Danube at that time. For Constantine, he had captured the significant cities of the Balkans and extended his sphere of influence almost to the Hellespont.

The two emperors had formerly been political and military allies, although perhaps not quite friends. They had shared a mutually beneficial alliance against their now defeated enemies. Without common enemies, and without the expediency of the proverb 'my enemy's enemy is my friend', there was nothing now binding them together. Their mutual rivalry was evident, and probably felt more by Licinius than Constantine because of his recent defeats in battle.

The next seven years were characterised by a peace of sorts. There was no open conflict between the two, but there was an ever-present tension on the border between the two rival halves of the empire. At the beginning of this period, Licinius moved his capital to Nicomedia from Sirmium; this was an act born of necessity because of the loss of all of his major cities in the Balkans. This city was to act as Licinius' base of operations for the remainder of this *inter bellum*. Constantine also moved his base from Trier further east to Serdica (modern Sofia). This was less out of necessity and more to control the Balkans that had recently come into his possession. As soon as he was of age, Crispus (the new western Caesar) was stationed at Trier to control the always-troublesome Rhine frontier and fill the power vacuum that had inevitable been left by Constantine's move further east.

Chapter 8

Resumption of War: Adrianople, Byzantium and Chrysopolis

Throughout the *inter bellum*, relations between the two emperors remained tense, but the peace did hold, however tenuous it may have been. The relationship between the two rivals took a decided turn for the worse when, in 320, Licinius began something of a purge of Christians in the east. It is alleged that he expelled Christians from imperial service, banished some from the empire, took possession of the property of others, banned synods and perhaps even ordered the deaths of some of the most devout. Eusebius tells us (set after Licinius' final defeat) that Constantine returned home to the backdrop of persecution:

> ... those who for refusing to worship idols had been sentenced to banishment and expulsion by the governors of provinces. Next they released from their obligations those who had on the same grounds been enrolled among the *curiales*, and summoned those deprived of property to resume it. Those who at the time of trial distinguished themselves by their fortitude in the cause of God, and had been sent to hard labour mines, or sentenced to live on islands, or compelled to servile labour on public works, enjoyed absolute release from them all.[1]

Given Constantine's (by this time not-so-new) faith, these alleged acts of Licinius (that is, assuming there was some form of persecution of Christians) would have been impossible to simply stand by and watch from the safety of the western empire.

From 317 Constantine had been building and securing his political base in the west, and he was using his religious beliefs as a means of achieving this. He had taken on a number of Christian leaders as advisors, had studied

Christian texts extensively and was increasingly intervening in the general affairs of the nascent church.[2] He had also begun something of a public relations campaign. He evidently realised that his personal beliefs could only take him and the empire so far; what was needed was more of a public effort. So he progressively made those beliefs known and correspondingly they increasingly informed his public decision-making. Constantine began to portray his civil war against Maxentius as divinely inspired. He started to depict Maxentius as an oppressor of Christians, and that his war was motivated by the desire to protect them. Historically speaking, this is a case of reading meaning into past events in the light of the present. Maxentius was well-known for his tolerance of Christians, but as we all know, and unfortunately for Maxentius, history is written by the victor.[3]

Throughout this supposedly peaceful period, relations between the two men continued steadily downhill. By 321 both parties refused to recognise the legitimacy of the consular appointments of the other.[4] With a declining relationship, and either side seemingly unwilling to compromise with the other, a clash was in the making. Both sides seem to have seen this as inevitable and both realised that funds would be necessary to conduct the coming conflict (money being the sinews of war), and both sides were apparently very short of the required funds. In 321, an empire-wide census was conducted; the actions of both emperors are telling of their respective levels of ability.

Constantine created a new imperial officeholder with the title *peraequator census* whose role appears to have been to assess the tax owed by citizens, and to hear appeals against taxation unfairly demanded from the state:

> When others complained about the land measurements made under previous rulers, alleging that their estates were overburdened, once again in this case by a decree he sent adjustment officers [*peraequatores*] to provide relief to the petitioners.[5]

Constantine seemingly attempted to make the system fairer and more transparent, although we do not know how many appeals went in favour of the regular citizen taxpayer. Constantine succeeded in increasing the total tax revenue whilst attempting to maintain the sound taxation principle that the burden should be shared around and not placed disproportionately on any one sector of the citizenry (a sure recipe for discontent).[6]

Licinius' approach to an empty treasury was rather different. Not-withstanding Eusebius' anti-Licinius rhetoric, which makes it hard to know precisely what his taxation policies were, it does appear that he had a radical reassessment of property values and increased the age at which exemption from property tax was allowed:

Thus he devised new land measurements, so that the smallest plot should be reckoned greater in size, out of greed for extra taxation. Thus also he registered persons who were no longer on estates but long since dead and buried, making this a source of further profit to himself.[7]

The source evidence seems to suggest that the age at which exemption from this tax came in to force was raised to 70, and retired soldiers also had their exemptions removed. These were policies that were repealed by Constantine after his final victory, but for the time being in the eastern empire, the taxation system was seen as punitive and excessive.[8]

Constantine's approach to these issues had been subtle and had the net effect of raising taxation without anyone noticing that they were paying more, and without feeling the pinch, a tricky proposition for any government (then and now). Licinius, on the other hand, had a more brutal approach that wasn't good for his image, because it seemed to be punitive across the board. In this, Constantine showed himself to be a politician of some ability, but Licinius was not.

In 322 Constantine was again campaigning, but not yet against Licinius. The Sarmatians had launched a sizeable raid into Roman territory across the Danube and had sacked several major cities in the region. The ability of this invading tribe to cross the frontier and cause the mischief they did before Constantine could react is interesting on several fronts. Firstly, it illustrates very clearly that the *limitanei* were particularly weak along this section of the frontier. This could be because they were poor quality troops, but more likely it was because Constantine had stripped these frontiers of men of age, but more than was safe to bolster his *comitatenses* for the coming civil war. Barbarian tribes typically attempted raiding missions when they perceived a weakness along the border, and this Sarmatian threat was probably no different to all the others past and future.

Constantine apparently did not respond with overwhelming alacrity, and we must consider why. Nevertheless, it is true to say that he did respond and he drove the barbarians out of Roman territory, but not before they could sack a number of key cities. It could be that he was worried about the threat from the east, or more likely that his field army was still not strong. His tax income from the previous year would have been used to bolster the army, but new troops needed training and equipping and that was likely ongoing at the time of the Sarmatian invasion. Either way, when Constantine did act, his actions were swift and decisive. He led the army himself and drove the barbarians from the region, and Zosimus narrates these events (which also tell us something about Roman siege-craft, to be discussed later) as follows:

> When Constantine learned that the Sarmatians, who live near Lake Maeotis, had sailed across the Danube and were pillaging his territory, he led his army against them. The barbarians resisted under their king Rausimodus and first attacked a strongly garrisoned town, the wall of which was built of stone, except for the very top which was wood. The Sarmatians, expecting to capture the town easily if they burnt the wooden part of the wall, set it alight and fired at those on top, but the defenders upon the walls threw down missiles and stones with deadly effect, and when Constantine came up and fell on them from the rear, he killed many, took more prisoners and put the rest to flight. Now that Rausimodus had lost most of his army, he embarked and crossed back over the Danube with the intention of later ravaging Roman territory again. On discovering this Constantine followed, and crossing the Danube himself, attacked the barbarians as they fled to a thick wood on a hill. Many were killed, including Rausimodus himself, but he also took many alive and spared the rest who sought mercy. So he returned to his headquarters with many captives.[9]

Constantine made good political capital out of the victory, advertising it on coins minted shortly afterwards.[10] These coins were a sign of the continuing breakdown in the relationship between the two emperors, and Licinius refused to distribute them in the east. It could well be that Licinius did not want to advertise so openly to his own citizens that Constantine was militarily strong and was still gaining victories against barbarian opposition. To the citizenry, Constantine may have looked like a better bet if they had been given all the facts on which to base their judgement.

After his victory against the Sarmatians, Constantine was riding high, and in the following year he was again faced with a barbarian threat, this time in Licinian-controlled Thrace. A tribe of Goths had made an incursion into Thrace, and whilst this was nominally in Licinian territory, Licinius actually had very few troops in that sector beyond the frontier garrisons. These garrisons again proved themselves to be ineffective at preventing an invasion, and their major purpose was probably to deter minor invasions. Licinius' mobile field army was stationed with him at Nicomedia some distance away from Thrace.

This invasion presented Constantine with a golden opportunity. He could invade and occupy the remainder of the European empire that was still under Licinius' control under the pretext of repelling the barbarian invasion.[11] It is unlikely that Constantine genuinely feared that the invaders would turn their attention to the west and perhaps invade Italy, he certainly had enough troops to make this almost impossible and the only real conclusion is that this was either a good pretext for war with Licinius or a land grab on the part of Constantine. There is actually no positive evidence for this Gothic invasion, and many assume it to be conflated with the earlier Sarmatian invasion; whatever the reality, the incursion by Constantine into Licinian territory seems beyond doubt. Licinius was outraged by Constantine's actions. In reality there should have been little wrong with two emperors aiding each other militarily for the good of the whole empire, but they just did not see it this way.

Once the Goths had been driven from Thrace, and no doubt after Constantine had done as much as he possibly could to make himself look like the one true legitimate emperor to the populace of the region, he returned to Thessaloniki on the coast in the autumn of 323. Constantine's plans for war with Licinius were delayed, and with winter approaching and a campaign that late in the season problematic, Constantine spent the winter regrouping with his son Crispus, who arrived with a significant proportion of his own field army, and they spent the winter of 323 finalising their plans for the conquest of the eastern empire.

The winter of 323/4 passed without incident, but the western emperor and his subordinates in Thessaloniki had been anything but idle, since they had been given orders to make good the harbour in Thessaloniki so it could accommodate a massively improved fleet, and Zosimus records that:

> Upwards of two hundred triaconters were built, and more than two thousand transports, one hundred and twenty thousand infantry, and ten thousand each of seamen and cavalry were assembled.[12]

Furthermore:

> When the land and sea forces of each [Constantine and Licinius] were thus organised and Licinius was camped at Hadrianople in Thrace, Constantine sent for his navy, which was mostly Greek, from the Piraeus. Then he [Constantine] advanced from Thessalonica with his infantry and camped on the bank of the Hebrus river.[13]

In the spring of 324 Constantine retraced his steps to Thessaloniki with the majority of his field army, accompanied by Crispus who was to take command of the fleet. At that city he was met by a large force gathered by his local sub-commanders. Zosimus tells us that Constantine now commanded 120,000 men, 10,000 cavalry and a huge fleet of ships, some 200 strong:

After distributing these [captives of war] among various cities, he came to Thessalonica where he built a harbour, which it did not have before. He then prepared again for war with Licinius. Upwards of two hundred triaconters were built, and more than two thousand transports, one hundred and twenty thousand infantry, and ten thousand each of seamen and cavalry were assembled. When Licinius heard of Constantine's preparations, he sent messengers throughout his realm bidding them make ready war-ships, infantry and cavalry. The Egyptians immediately sent eighty triremes, the Phoenicians as many more, the Ionians and Dorians in Asia sixty, the Cyprians thirty, the Carians twenty, the Bithynians thirty, and the Africans fifty; his infantry numbered one hundred and fifty thousand, and his cavalry, supplied by Phrygia and Cappadocia, fifteen thousand. Constantine's ships were at anchor in the Piraeus, Licinius' in the Hellespont.[14]

As indicated, this fleet, although enormous, was not entirely made up of warships; there were many transport vessels which were of every size and shape; large numbers of warships must also have been present, however, as the later siege of Byzantium suggests. Their intention was to aid the eastward advance rather than to create or ensure the naval supremacy of the western emperor.[15] Constantine also had a second fleet gathered at Piraeus, the port of Athens, a strategically important location from which to open a second front on Licinius' flanks, or to prevent Licinius doing the same against the west.

However history may judge Licinius, he did see the writing on the wall and made his own preparations for the inevitable war. He also gathered together an army that was even larger than that commanded by Constantine, and Zosimus has told us of the size of Licinius' force: 150,000 men, 15,000 cavalry and 350 warships. It is difficult to fathom where these troops came from after a series of defeats in recent years, but we can speculate that the majority were recently enrolled into the army and therefore not as well trained, and certainly not as experienced as those commanded by Constantine and Crispus. Eusebius tells us of Licinius' preparations, with all of his usual prejudice:

Yet he again began to assemble a military force in secret, once more he initiated war and battle, called barbarian men to his support, and went about looking for other gods, since he had been deceived by the previous ones.[16]

There would certainly have been a core of veterans, but these had been defeated several times by Constantine and this would have had a significant detrimental impact on their moral and reliability. In short, Constantine's men expected to be victorious, Licinius' veterans had already tasted defeat. In order to counter the Constantinian fleet, Licinius also gathered his own which he stationed in the Hellespont to support his flanks.

Licinius' strategy for the coming war was fundamentally defensive, his actions clearly demonstrate that he did not want to move far from his power base, and did not want to risk lengthy lines of supply and communication. He also ensured his flanks were protected, firstly by the frontier forces along the Danube, and secondly by the fleet in the northern Aegean, commanded by Abantus, patrolling the south coast of Thrace and the Hellespont. This was a fairly sound strategy for a commander who has been recently defeated several times, and who would not want to risk being outflanked by Constantine, who had the capability to divide his forces between himself and Crispus, if he advanced too far beyond the border with the west.

Constantine's strategy was entirely the opposite, however. Constantine and Crispus devised a two pronged assault against Licinius. Constantine would advance at the head of the majority of the army directly eastwards whilst Crispus would take command of the fleet and sail for the Hellespont and Byzantium:

> Now with the peace having been broken between the two [Licinius and Constantine], by agreement Constantine sent Caesar Crispus with a large fleet to invade Asia.[17]

Given that a significant proportion of the fleet gathered at Thessaloniki were transport vessels, a significant part of the field army would have embarked on them with the aim of either landing somewhere along the Thracian coast, or close to Byzantium to outflank Licinius' position, exactly what the latter was hoping to avoid by staying in friendly territory.

In the spring of 324 Licinius, with his newly reformed army, marched westwards and made camp close to Adrianople on the eastern banks of the Hebrus River (the larger of the two rivers close to Adrianople).[18] The Hebrus River flows from the northwest of Thrace and along the southern side of Adrianople where it merges with the smaller Tonoseius River, and the combined larger body of water flows south and empties into the northern Aegean close to Samothrace.

Licinius' deployment again suggests the fundamentally defensive nature of his strategy as this was an excellent defensive position. Once stationed, Licinius' men prepared their positions and awaited the enemy. Constantine's strategy was dictated to him by Licinius' movements. The western emperor could not possible allow a numerically larger enemy force to go undefeated, and he could not risk any movement against Licinius' territory that did not first involve defeating his eastern counterpart once again. Constantine needed to cross the Hellespont to conquer the eastern empire, but first he needed to capture Byzantium and Adrianople, and to achieve the latter he had to defeat Licinius.

Constantine marched northeast from Thessaloniki in spring of 324 into Thrace and into Licinius-controlled territory. He did not march swiftly, but they did go directly towards Adrianople and the waiting enemy. When Constantine arrived at the Hebrus River, he found Licinius already en-camped on the eastern bank and waiting his arrival. Hostilities did not commence immediately, but there appears to have been a lengthy delay as both sides made every effort not to be the one to make the first mistake. For Licinius, his defensive strategy was suited to a lengthy delay, and he would have had no difficulties with supply as he was close to the Black Sea and the Hellespont, both of which were under his control.

Constantine seems unusually cautious at this point; he simply dug himself in and awaited events. The delay could be something of a timing issue with the fleet, perhaps he was waiting for news that the Piraeus fleet was either on its way or close by, or perhaps he was simply trying to figure out a tactic that would allow him to cross this substantial river and achieve victory with minimal losses. Licinius' troops had been arrayed in a lengthy battle line to make a flanking manoeuvre as difficult as possible for Constantine. Constantine matched the Licinian dispositions as far as he could, in spite of his smaller army.[19]

For an unspecified period of time, but what was most likely a few weeks, Constantine attempted to make preparations for a direct frontal assault. This was perhaps a ruse and no frontal assault was intended; the Hebrus River is deep and wide, so this would have been extremely difficult to say the least. The preparations were probably as much to see if he could provoke some kind of reaction from Licinius or his troops that he could exploit (a gap in Licinius' line, for example). This did not occur however. The tactic was perhaps also to keep the enemy alert and awake, to prevent them from resting properly during the phony war period so that eventually they would get complacent and not react quickly when the real strike did finally arrive.

After another unspecified period, but it seems to be a couple of weeks rather than just a few days, Constantine issued an order for one of his flanks to start to fell trees in their sector and make preparations for the construction of a bridge that would allow a safe crossing of the river. If the bridge had been constructed it would have allowed a crossing in force at that point against Licinius' flank. After a few days of this, with enough time to allow the defenders to see exactly what Constantine's forces were doing, Constantine ordered around 5,000 infantry and archers, along with 800 cavalry to with-draw from the front line and take up a position in a wooded area on the opposite end of the line from where the bridge was being constructed. This could not have been easy to hide and must have involved troops from several legions otherwise the troop movement would have been too obvious, and a significant gap in the line would have opened up revealing that a secondary tactic was underway.

At dawn on 3 July Constantine led these concealed troops across a fordable section of the Hebrus River at the opposite end of the line from the bridge construction. Zosimus explains how Constantine devised this tactic:

> The armies lay against each other like this [extended over several stades] for several days, until Constantine, noticing where the river was narrowest, devised the following scheme. He ordered his soldiers to bring down wood from the mountain and bind it with rope as if he intended to bridge the river and take his army across. Having thus deceived the enemy, he ascended a hill which had thick woods capable of hiding anyone and planted five thousand infantry and archers and eight hundred cavalry there. Then, taking twelve horsemen, he crossed the Hebrus at its narrowest, most fordable part and fell on the enemy unawares.[20]

This surprise attack caught the enemy completely off guard, and although they had well-prepared defensive positions, they did not have long to form up and resist the crossing before Constantine's men were upon them, led by Constantine himself. Licinius' troops would have been preparing to defend the point where the bridge construction was occurring, and so they had strengthened the sector of the line where this attack was occurring, but this was at the expense of other parts of battle (most likely the centre where nothing of significance had happened for some time).

Once the commanders in the centre saw some of the Licinian forces being redeployed, they began their own crossing of the central sections of the river. This must have been on an earlier order from Constantine. He must have expected that Licinius would move to support his threatened flank, and when this occurred the troops in the centre were to begin their attack. The fighting was fierce and prolonged with each side faring differently in different sectors. As Constantine had done in earlier battles, he had a detach-ment of his own guards carry his standard (which was becoming something of a talisman) into the battle.

The battle raged all day and into the evening. The very length of the battle suggests that the Licinian forces recovered their wits quickly and that both sides fought vigorously, no quarter asked or given. The decisive moment in the battle was a cavalry charge by Constantine which occurred in the early evening. This charge finally broke the enemy lines, and it was an action in which Constantine himself was wounded. This final charge forced the realisation on Licinius that he had been defeated once again. As night fell, Licinius fled east towards Byzantium with as many troops as he could rapidly gather together.

Licinius left significant numbers of his own men dead on the field of battle. Zosimus reports 30,000 dead (a suspiciously large number, but this is the case with most casualty figures from the ancient world).[21] After the battle, Constantine immediately moved on Adrianople and received its surrender without incident. He also received the surrender of many thousands of Licinius' troops who had been stationed there, as well as many whom he had just defeated on the field of battle. This desertion by Licinius' forces was a triple blow to the eastern emperor. He had lost the battle, he had lost the remains of his western empire and he had lost most of his army. Licinius had no choice but to flee the field of battle. He first moved south east as fast as he could and reached Byzantium. From there he boarded ship (Abantus was patrolling the area) and headed into Bithynia in Asia Minor.

Licinius knew that his western possessions were now lost for good, but he was still confident in containing Constantine in Europe and not allowing him to cross the Hellespont into Asia. This would be achieved by means of Abantus' fleet containing that of Crispus. It also required Constantine to be pinned in Europe by Licinius' forces in Byzantium and on the mainland. Licinius was not yet finally defeated.[22] Licinius knew that if he could reach Asia Minor with a significant enough number of troops, and if all else failed he would still have some troops in Asia Minor with which to oppose an invasion of his heartlands by Constantine. Their reliability must, by now, be brought seriously into question. These remaining troops would likely be his most loyal veterans, but they had been defeated in every encounter with the western emperor and there was no reason to think that they or their commander had the necessary military skills to defeat Constantine.

After success in the battle, Constantine quickly captured the city of Adrianople and immediately afterwards gave chase to the fleeing Licinius. He also sent orders to Crispus to attack the enemy fleet and drive it from the strategically important Hellespont region. If successful, this would allow the western emperor to besiege Byzantium with a reasonable expectation of success, once the possibility of resupply and reinforcement from Asia Minor had been removed. Therefore, Constantine's actions at Byzantium and the

Hellespont indicate that he was now fully determined to eliminate the ever-present threat posed by Licinius once and for all. However, the city was just as determined to remain loyal to Licinius and made ready to resist the conqueror. Its walls were strong and sturdy, and the defensive force was significant. They were also well-supplied.

Constantine arrived at the city and quickly realised that the prospective siege would not be quick. He had hoped that the populace would welcome him with open arms, but for whatever reason they remained loyal to Licinius. Constantine made camp to the west of the city and began preparations. The legions began be constructing an earthwork against one of the walls of the city. This tactic sounds oddly similar to some of the accounts of Alexander the Great's siege of Gaza in 332.[23] This earthwork would have looked like a huge ramp leading to (or close to) the top of the walls of the city. Once this was complete a siege tower was dragged to the top of the ramp to provide fire to suppress the defenders as the assault began in earnest; though in a later chapter a fuller picture of Roman siegecraft is given.

The earthwork must have been completed under intolerable fire from the defenders. As the workmen drew closer to the walls they would have been sitting ducks for the archers (and perhaps slingers) inside the fortress. It seems most probable, in that case, that the ramp was not complete at the time the siege tower was dragged to its summit. The ramp would have been close enough for archers and slingers to lay down a suppressing fire against the defenders. With this defensive fire in place, the construction workers could complete the ramp and the assault of the city proper could begin.

This build-up to the point where the assault could begin in earnest would not have been quick. Even with the legendary efficiency of the Roman army, it is hard to see how such a major earthwork construction could have been accomplished in less than a couple of months. This was enough time for Crispus to get his navy in a position to act against the Licinian fleet defending the Hellespont. Constantine would have wanted Crispus to attack the defending fleet at the same time as he was commencing his attacks against the walls as a two pronged attack to take pressure away from the sector in which he was concentrating his assault. It is further likely that he would have made small scale assaults against other sections of the walls, not with the intention of actually breaking through, but with the aim of distracting the defenders and forcing them to divide their forces and prevent them from concentrating against the main thrust of the attack.

Crispus' assault against the defenders of the Hellespont was initially small scale. He used only 80 warships in his initial assault; this fleet was challenging a defending force of around 200 vessels.[24] The defenders felt that they would have been able to surround and overwhelm such a small force given the disparity in numbers, and in a normal naval battle this would have been true. This naval battle was more Salamis than Actium, however, and the large numbers of the defending fleet actually was their Achilles heel in the context of the narrows of the Hellespont. Crispus was able to out-manoeuvre the defending ships, ram many in the flanks and sink significant numbers. Abantus was a wise enough commander to see what was happening and to realise his mistake. Once he had, he withdrew his remaining forces to the eastern end of the Hellespont to regroup, resupply and gather what limited reinforcements were available in the Black Sea.

Crispus used the lull in the fighting equally productively. Much of his fleet had been left outside of the Hellespont as they would only have hindered Crispus' tactic. These were now brought up to support Constantine's admiral and final preparations were made for what would be the decisive engagement at sea, and the day after the initial skirmish the final battle was fought. We have limited information on the tactics of the battle, but we do know it was vicious and decisive. The weather in the region played a significant factor in the victory. Many of the Licinian ships were blown onto the rocks near where they had been stationed and many sailors' lives were lost to the sea as a result. Those that escaped this fate were hunted down and destroyed ruthlessly and relentlessly by the fleet of Crispus. Apparently only four of Licinius' vessels escaped destruction or capture. Even the warship commanded by Abantus himself was sunk and he only just escaped with his life.[25]

After the battle, Crispus quickly loaded his fleet with supplies and made for the Bosporus to relieve the besieging forces. The results of the naval battle, and the sudden arrival of a hostile fleet, would have made the lot of the defenders of Byzantium all but impossible. Their potential means of escape was now removed. Their supply lines had been severed and there was no hope of reinforcements. They were on their own.

Once the defenders were under threat from two sides and all hope of relief gone, they surrendered to the western emperor. Constantine and Crispus marched victorious into the last city to hold out against the western emperor. Licinius was defeated yet again, but yet again he did not admit that the struggle was finally over. He retreated to Chalcedon and raised yet another army. This new army centred on the core of veterans that had survived from his mobile field army that had been decisively defeated in eastern Europe. Licinius also gathered troops still loyal to him from the eastern empire, stripping the frontier forces in the process. In addition he used his wealth accumulated from the east to hire a large force of Gothic mercenaries. This new force quickly became of a size that Licinius felt capable of defeating Constantine. Whether it was of sufficient quality was an entirely separate question, however.

As a further measure, Licinius promoted Martinianus to the rank of Augustus and gave him command of a large body of men. Martinianus was dispatched to Lampsacus with orders to patrol the eastern shoreline and prevent a crossing in force by Constantine's troops. If Licinius could maintain Fortress Asia Minor for long enough, he had resources sufficient to gather and train a much larger and more powerful army than that which he currently commanded and could potentially take back the territory he had recently lost.

Martinianus' troops would have mainly consisted of cavalry. He needed men who were mobile and could quickly react to an attempted crossing. They would have needed to patrol up and down the coast on a daily basis. The force would have been quite large, but not particularly powerful, but it did not need to be. All Martinianus needed to do was repel an attempted crossing, and as long as he had the advantage of dry land, and assuming he caught the enemy before they were fully disembarked, then his task was achievable with a reactive force consisting mainly of cavalry. His main objective was to buy time for Licinius to muster, and, more importantly, to train a sizeable army for what was likely to be the decisive encounter.

Martinianus' problem was quite simple. The coastline was very extensive and replete with very many coves and inlets. It was simply impossible for him to patrol the entire length of the coast from the Bosporus to the Hellespont as would have been required by Licinius' strategy. If this strategy were to have any chance of success it would have taken several 'battle groups' operating in different sectors, each suitably equipped with cavalry and scouts. It would also have taken at least a semblance of a fleet to patrol the Sea of Marmara and constantly scout out the positions of the enemy fleet. As it was, Martinianus did the best he could with the limited resources at his disposal.

Constantine was aware of Martinianus' tactic to prevent his landing and he needed an idea of how to overcome it. Despite the difficulties of the task assigned to Martinianus, his presence and his patrols did make it risky and difficult to force a landing in hostile territory while opposed. Constantine's answer was a classic tactic of misdirection. He ordered elements of his sizeable fleet of warships to move up and down the coast whilst also gathering together a fleet of smaller transport vessels. The warships commanded by Crispus were far from ideally suited to a naval landing, but Martinianus could not take the risk and had to keep patrolling up and down the coastline. While the navy was doing this, Constantine boarded his troops on the small transport vessels and crossed unopposed, landing at a place called the Sacred Promontory, only 35km from Licinius' own position in Chalcedon:

> While Licinius was thus engaged, [posting his forces on the hills and valleys around Chalcedon] Constantine had a great number of vessels, both transports and warships, which he wished to use to gain control of the opposite shore, but he feared that the Bithynian coast would be inaccessible especially to transports. So he built galleys and swift-sailing skiffs and sailed to the so-called Sacred Promontory, which lies at the mouth of the Black Sea, two hundred stades from Chalcedon. There he landed his army and went up to some hills from which he extended his battle line.[26]

Martinianus had failed, but his task was an impossible one. Licinius was now in a very precarious position. He commanded an army of significant size, but it was largely untried; it was an army which would have benefited greatly from a few months of training, but the enemy was only 35km away. Licinius immediately summoned Martinianus and his vital detachments of troops, but they were 400km distant and unlikely to reach Licinius' position in Chalcedon in time to have an impact on the coming battle.[27] Since Licinius felt that he could not wait for reinforcements from Martinianus, he gathered his troops outside Chalcedon. As soon as he was able he marched towards Constantine with every intention of forcing a conclusion to the civil war that had been raging for some years. Licinius did not have to march far; he arrived at Chrysopolis which is now Üsküdar in modern-day Turkey.

In previous battles Licinius was always the one who arrived first on the battlefield and set up a defensive position, thus choosing the ground upon which he was to fight; not that it had done him any good to this point. At Chrysopolis he did not have this luxury. He arrived to find Constantine already in position and awaiting his arrival. Constantine was in no hurry, the longer he waited in his bridgehead the more troops he could get across the Bosporus. Constantine could afford to wait, Licinius could not; he needed to fight the battle before the odds were stacked so far against him that he would have no chance of victory. Therefore, given the situation, Licinius sensibly chose to attack rather than sitting back and allowing his enemy to take the strategic advantage from him.

On 18 September 324 Licinius and Constantine set their men up on the battlefield for what would prove to be the final battle in this bloody and vicious civil war. Constantine, as was now usual, had the religious standard move along his lines to support his troops where it was required. Licinius had become terribly superstitious over the power of this standard and instructed his troops not to look directly at it, lest some disaster befell them.

Constantine's tactic for the battle was brutally simple but remarkable effective. Constantine simply ordered a massive central assault against the middle of the enemy lines. This was the sledgehammer approach to warfare: there was absolutely no guile whatsoever in this tactic. Rather, Constantine reasoned that his troops had defeated Licinius' several times now and that there was no need for a well thought out battle plan. Licinius, on the other hand, seems to have taken a defensive posture immediately upon setting up his lines. He may have arrived late at the battlefield, but his defensive tactics were still in evidence. Zosimus describes the nature of the battle and its aftermath:

> A sharp battle took place between Chalcedon and the Sacred Promontory, which Constantine won convincingly; for he attacked the enemy vigorously and wrought such slaughter that scarcely thirty thousand out of one hundred and thirty thousand escaped. As soon as this was known to the Byzantines, they threw open their gates to welcome Constantine, and the Chalcedonians did the same. After this defeat, Licinius retreated to Nicomedia with his surviving cavalry and a few thousand infantry.[28]

What seems to have happened is that Constantine's men attacked the centre of Licinius' line and broke through very quickly. Understandably enough, Licinius' troops had no real stomach for a fight by this time, and they fell in their tens of thousands to Constantine's men. We are told that 25,000 Licinian soldiers were killed, and an unknown number of Constantine's. As always when we have to rely on ancient sources, these figures are difficult to believe because contemporary ancient historians tend to exaggerate in their reporting.

Licinius managed to flee the field of battle once again, heading for the relative safety of Nicomedia. By this time, it looked pretty hopeless for the eastern emperor. He had been defeated on more than one occasion by Constantine. His army had been shattered, reformed and then shattered again. His mobile field army was defeated and his frontier was stripped right down. He was in a much worse financial position than he had been several years previously and, therefore, the hopes of raising a mercenary army were severely diminished (and that is even if Constantine had given him respite from attack).

Now desperate, defeated and on the run, Licinius was out of options. His wife, Constantia, persuaded him to throw himself on the mercy of her brother. Constantia's plan, however, was not so simple as to suggest that Licinius ought to walk into Constantine's camp and abase himself and throw himself down at the feet of the victor. Constantia herself acted as an emissary and went to see her brother herself to seek leniency on behalf of her husband. Constantia's offer was quite simple: Licinius and Martinianus would immediately surrender on one condition only: that their lives would be spared.

Perhaps fearing further guerrilla warfare if he were forced to chase down Licinius, or perhaps simply viewing an act of leniency as an appropriate way to end a civil war and begin to build bridges from east to west, or perhaps simply because it was his sister who had asked and he was sensitive to the familial ties, Constantine accepted the offer immediately. Upon receiving the answer that she wanted, Constantia returned to Nicomedia where she delivered the message. Later that same day, Licinius and Martinianus travelled the short distance to Constantine's camp where they surrendered their purple vestments and saluted Constantine as the sole emperor of a recently reunified Roman Empire.

Upon their surrender, Licinius and Martinianus were separated. Licinius was escorted by armed guards to Thessaloniki, where he was forced to retire from public life. Martinianus was removed to Cappadocia and the same fate befell him immediately. Their retirement was probably fairly comfortable, but their access to public life and to visitors from the world of men and affairs would have been severely restricted. This being said, Constantine had at least kept his word to his sister that the two would not be killed.

Though it turned out that Constantine's word was not of indefinite length. The year after their capture and virtual imprisonment, there were allegations against both of conspiracy and plotting against the emperor. It is impossible to say with any certainty from this distance (and given the bias in those sources that might wish to tar Licinius) whether the allegations had any validity, but Constantine obviously felt justified in breaking his promise to Constantia and subsequently had both men executed. This is also perhaps an indication that within only the short space of a year, the eastern empire was not considered a flashpoint any longer, and Constantine felt comfortable in exercising his authority without fear of serious retribution.

The Roman Empire was again united under a sole ruler. It was not immediately obvious that east and west could coexist peacefully after a period of division and civil strife. Constantine's quick and decisive act of leniency towards the defeated former eastern emperor was a cleverly designed act to begin to heal the divisions that had been cut between the two sides of the Roman Empire.[29] On a strategic level, one of Constantine's first acts had to be to rebuild the eastern empire on the military front. Licinius' campaigns had left the east perilously weak and the frontier now needed to be built up again as a matter of urgency. The situation in the west was nowhere near as bad, but even so the resources of the west had been depleted in order to ensure victory. Moreover, with the benefit of hindsight, the victory also meant something rather momentous: the empire was now solely ruled by a Christian; the first Christian emperor. Bearing in mind that the change to Christianity was slow, and was nowhere near as sudden and decisive as Eusebius makes out, he commemorates the importance of this military achievement by stating:

> Now that the evil men were removed, the sunlight shone, purified at last of dictatorial tyranny. The whole Roman dominion was joined together, the peoples of the east being united with the other half, and the whole body was orderly disposed by the single universal government acting as its head, the authority of a single ruler reaching every part. Bright beams of the light of true religion brought shining days to those who before had 'sat in darkness and the shadow of death' (Luke 1:79; Isaiah 9:1). There was no more memory of former evils, as all people everywhere sang praise to the victor and professed to know only his saviour god.[30]

In terms of its significance as a historical moment, Constantine's victory at Chrysopolis, all made possible by his military strategy and generalship, was a still moment in the turning forces of social, cultural and religious transformation that were currently churning about the Roman world. Even Zosimus concurs:

> The whole empire now devolved on Constantine alone. At last he no longer needed to conceal his natural malignity but acted in accordance with his unlimited power.[31]

Chapter 9

Imperial Reorganisation and the Final Campaigns

After the final defeat of Licinius, Constantine was keen to get started on a series of reforms. In what must have been one of his very first acts as the new emperor, Constantine ordered the refounding of an old city, one that would bear his name. This was to be: Constantinople (taken from his name and the Greek for city: *polis*). This new city was founded on the site of the ancient city of Byzantium, but it was laid out to be far grander and would become far more powerful than its predecessor (an eastern backwater) had ever been.

The actual events surrounding the founding of the city have become shrouded by the mists of time, and it is far from clear what Constantine's long term plans were for his new foundation. Did he intend to move the capital from the very first? Constantine appears to have begun the construction of the new city around November 324, almost immediately after the surrender of Licinius.[1] Byzantium, and therefore Constantinople also, was remarkably well located. It occupied a key location between east and west and was essentially the gateway for anyone travelling either to or fro. It was also brilliantly situated to control the Danube frontier to the northwest and the Armenia region to the northeast. A strong garrison could aid in keeping both (potentially difficult) areas under control. It was a very easy city to reinforce and resupply if it ever came under siege, assuming the defenders could maintain naval hegemony.

Lastly, it controlled the Bosporus Straights and therefore controlled the grain supply coming out of the Black Sea, and this was the grain supply necessary to sustain the urban environment in the first place. It really cannot be overstated how important this final point is. The ruler of Constantinople could go a long way into starving Rome, or any other major city, into submission if he so wished: with such powerful leverage at his disposal the possibilities were immense. With hindsight, we can perhaps suspect that Constantine had every intention of moving his capital from a very early stage. Constantine had only rarely been stationed in Rome, and the city would not have had the same historical pull on him as it did for so many of his early counterparts. The idea of moving the capital would not have been outlandish or even all that iconoclastic to contemplate for an emperor who had had very little relationship with the traditional capital in the first place. Indeed, it is true to say that most men who had held the imperial position since around 290 had had their own capital cities, although admittedly they were still within the framework of Rome remaining the major urban administrative and political centre.[2]

But Constantine was no fool. He had captured Byzantium with relative ease. The walls were easy to breach, and once he had achieved naval superiority then the city could be blockaded and pressure could simultaneously be brought to bear from a number of aspects. If Constantinople was indeed to become the new capital then it needed to be strengthened and fortified in accordance with the status of an imperial capital. The city would not be declared the new capital until it was ready, hence the delay after 324. It took almost six years of construction and preparation for Byzantium to be ready to take on its new lofty status, but on 11 May 330 a ceremony was held in the city at which it was formally dedicated as the new capital. Constantine himself was present at the celebrations, lending them even greater kudos than they may otherwise have commanded. His presence was crucial to the new city being accepted as the new capital, as was the fact that it took the emperor's name: this was, in a very real way, the 'city of Constantine', it was his city and the centre of his empire.

Constantine's refurbishment of the city was considerable. Along with much stronger and more extensive defensive fortifications (including very thick city walls) a new grid pattern for the street layout was introduced; a new imperial palace was constructed and the hippodrome extended and refurbished; a new and extensive bath complex was constructed; a grand forum, two major churches, a senate house and a capitol were also constructed and several temples to the old gods that had fallen into disrepair were also renewed and rebuilt. A new mint was also built in the new foundation to further highlight its new status as being on a par with Rome.[3] And just to make really sure that nobody forgot who was responsible for this massive project of rebuilding and extending, Constantine had a huge statue of himself erected on a plinth in the forum. The statue is of symbolic significance because it depicted the emperor holding a globe and a sceptre. It also depicted rays of the sun radiating out from his head.

There can be little doubt that these representations were intended to invoke in the observer the standard imagery of *Sol Invictus* (the Unconquered

Sun). This traditional pagan god representing victory was to become quite a favourite of Constantine, and was to appear on several coins minted during his reign. Many historians of the later Roman Empire interpret this syncretism as evidence that Constantine was insincere in his Christianity, or that he was communicating some deep internal conflict between old beliefs and new. A much simpler explanation seems more likely; was Constantine really the kind of deep thinker accustomed to making such multi-layered statements about the tensions between paganism and Christianity in his self-portrayal? Surely his use of pagan imagery only serves to remind us that paganism was still the main currency for imagery and representation in the Roman world.

Moreover, as a man used to realpolitik and its demands, Constantine would have been very used to keeping everybody onside. Using straight-forward pagan imagery of the *Sol Invictus* type would play well with the old guard; but Christianising it in other ways would have satisfied his own strong sense of duty and responsibility towards the Christian God and towards his associates and friends in the Christian community (not least, his mother Helena). Finally, it would have been natural for Constantine, who had imbibed the traditional art and cultural norms of the later Roman world from birth, to reach for those first in his self-presentation in statue. It would take a while longer for there to develop a distinctly Christian art and culture, one with its own norms and codes (such as the exquisite icons that pro-voked such theological controversy in later years). Certainly also there was expediency at work: there were still many pagans in the empire, and too overt a display of Christianity immediately upon his victory over Licinius might risk alienating large swathes of the empire, particularly in the east. The *Sol Invictus* symbolism also invoked Alexander the Great, who was fond of depicting himself with the ram horns of Zeus Ammon. In his symbolism, then, Constantine was still partly thinking like an old Roman, though some other of his actions spoke otherwise.

Interestingly, Constantine's relationship with his former patron deity, *Sol Invictus*, never entirely faded during his lifetime. This leads historians to question whether Constantine's faith was entirely genuine. His Christian faith had undoubtedly been a major factor in his victories over Licinius: the standard that was protected by a detachment of his bodyguards and moved around the battlefield to inspire the troops that were most in need is testimony to that. If Constantine had only been using his new found faith as an expedient tool to aid in the unification of the empire, then it was a good short-term move (undoubtedly the belief that the Christogram standard inspired boosted troop morale) but in the long-term a very poor choice indeed (though it would not be fair to blame Constantine for not foreseeing that). The early Church was soon beset with internal schism, theological disunity and debate (which Constantine tried his best to mediate between and to reconcile) and was certainly not a single united force overnight.[4]

In terms of his social policies, these were now informed by his religious affiliations. Members of the clergy, for example, were exempted from financial obligations to the state. This resulted (and perhaps this was always one of the intentions), in a greater enrolment in the church as a way of avoiding such financial obligations. Christianity was undeniably the new state religion, but paganism was not outlawed as such: it was allowed to fade gradually, and this was a much more effective way of avoiding civil unrest. Perhaps Constantine had learned a valuable lesson from the failures of the Christian persecutions. Christians were also favoured for promotion within the 'civil service' structure of the empire, and new positions were generally given to individuals who were demonstrably of that religion.

The new empire also needed a new 'Christian' governmental structure.[5] To achieve this, a new senate was formed in Constantinople and new senators were elected to fill its ranks. These senators were independent of Rome, and had no obligation whatsoever either to live in Rome or ever to attend the senate in Rome. Constantine also appointed new provincial governors who would be primarily loyal to the new emperor, rather than those who had served Licinius and others before him. These changes in administration were not immediate: he did not begin a wholesale removal of equestrians from positions of power, neither did he remove non-Christians, his administrative policies were far more subtle than this. These new appointments set in motion a new social system that saw the old equestrian class decline in importance besides the new senatorial class, although this took several generations to come to fruition and we don't know if Constantine ever had this as a long term goal, or if he was only ever planning for the short term.

Despite the slow pace of administrative change in the empire, the immediate changes for Constantine and his family were enormous. Constantine's family was of a significant size, and now that he was sole ruler he could get on with the Roman business-as-usual of nepotism, and so he put friends and family members in positions of power to help secure his own long term future. At the time of the defeat of Licinius, Constantine already had six children: two daughters and four sons. One of his sons, Crispus, had already been elected to the rank of Caesar and had played a major role in the capture of Byzantium and the final defeat of Licinius. Crispus also had many years of military experience from serving in Gaul. Another of Constantine's sons, Constantius II, had also been elected to the role of Caesar. In November 324, a third son was added to that exulted rank, Constantine II, demonstrating the pleasing, albeit also slightly annoying, later Roman habit of giving sons very similar names. Constantine also promoted two powerful imperial women to senior roles: his wife Fausta and his mother Helena (herself a devout Christian) were made Augustae.[6] Licinius' widow, Constantia achieved renewed status and influence (perhaps her earlier role as emissary and mediator between her husband and half-brother gives us a clue to her diplomatic talents) and she became something of a religious advisor to the emperor. This position was remarkably powerful, especially for a woman, and allowed her to have an input into most major policy decisions Constantine was to make during his reign.

Large families often bring difficulties, and Constantine's was no exception. According to one version, in the summer of 326 Constantine's wife, Fausta, approached her husband with a story that Crispus had attempted to rape her. Constantine reacted with violent rage. Crispus was a man of standing in the empire and was a military hero in his own right with potentially large numbers of troops in Gaul loyal to him. Constantine wasted no time in ordering Crispus' execution, apparently with little more than mere allegations against his son. At some point shortly after Crispus' death, Fausta admitted that the story had been fabricated. Constantine's rage was at least equal to that at the initial allegation and he ordered his wife's death too. She was bricked up in a bath house and the fires were stoked to such intensity that she was literally steamed alive:

> Without any consideration for natural law he killed his son Crispus, on suspicion of having had intercourse with his step-mother, Fausta. And when Constantine's mother, Helena, was saddened by this atrocity and was inconsolable at the young man's death, Constantine as if to comfort her, applied a remedy worse than the disease: he ordered a bath to be overheated, and shut Fausta up in it until she was dead.[7]

It is hard to imagine many more terrible fates. Whatever the reality of the reasons behind the executions, there seems little doubt that they actually occurred, and as Zosimus goes on to explain, the terrible guilt of these crimes weighed so heavily on Constantine that he sought any means of absolution possible, and in his telling it was for this reason that the ground was laid for his conversion to Christianity since it was offered to him as a way to easily expurgate him of his sin.[8]

Final Campaigns

After a period of respite and reorganisation at home, Constantine returned to the field of battle. In 328 he launched the largest attack against the lands of the barbarians for sixty years.[9] To facilitate this northern campaign, Constantine first built a massive stone bridge across the Danube. This bridge was around 2.5 km across and was likely the biggest bridge in the world at that time, and the longest ever built by the Romans.[10] The bridge was constructed at the settlement of Oescus and provided a 'highway' into barbarian territory. Any potential threat could now be quickly countered in barbarian lands rather than waiting until they were across the Danube before responding to the devastation that they were causing to Roman territory.

At the far end of the bridge, the Romans also constructed fortifications to protect the entrance into Roman territory, and perhaps just as importantly, to protect the bridge itself from barbarian attack. Bearing in mind that the Roman military mindset was almost exclusively offensive first and foremost, then these fortifications can be seen as this. As long as they were held, and the bridge was intact, the emperor could deposit tens of thousands of legionaries into Dacia very quickly and have them across the Danube and set up in formation before the enemy could even react.

For Constantine, and indeed other Roman emperors, Dacia was still something of a special place and it is no great surprise that the bridge was built to allow access to this former province. The region had been conquered by Trajan, but had later been abandoned by the emperor Aurelian in the late-third century. There seems little doubt that Constantine ultimately wanted to reverse that humiliation and recover the province. Constantine crossed the Danube and was victorious in a series of minor campaigns about which we know little. We do know, however, that the campaign did not progress far into Gothic lands before Constantine withdrew. Constantine had satisfied himself that he had given the barbarians a bloody nose; the full reconquest of Dacia would have to wait for another day.

Constantine also built a series of other fortifications along the Danube frontier. Although these were likely begun perhaps as early as 323, they were only completed at around the same time as the bridge over the Danube. This represented a significant upgrade in military capability for the Romans on this always-troublesome frontier. The Romans could now not only defend themselves more effectively (in theory at least), but they could also launch rapid pre-emptive strikes across the Danube without difficulty.

After these rapid attacks against the Gothic tribes, Constantine withdrew into Roman territory, but he was far from content to sit idle. In late 328 he moved to his former capital of Trier and issued a series of three laws that are commemorated in the Theodosian Code. The next two years were spent touring the region, before arriving back at Constantinople in mid-330 in time for its formal dedication.

At an unspecified point during this tour of the Rhine/Danube frontier, Constantine was taken by surprise and attacked by a large party of 500 heavily-armed Goth cavalry, who were the tribe of the Thaiphali. This tribe was a minor Gothic tribe and generally subordinate to the Tervingi who had not treated them well; it was probably this ill treatment that had forced them south across the Danube into Roman lands.[11] They were essentially caught between a rock and a hard place, and as with so many displaced peoples throughout history, they were down on their luck and with their backs against the wall.

The Thaiphali cavalry took Constantine's army completely by surprise. Zosimus tells us that a significant part of the Roman forces were killed and the Goths plundered much Roman territory, including the Roman field camp. He further tells us that Constantine was quite happy to escape with his life and flee the field of battle (implying cowardice and a failure of nerve). If true, this was clearly a major humiliation for Constantine, but it is one from which he recovered quickly. The defeat was likely not as serious as Zosimus implies, as the emperor appears to have driven out the invaders and re-secured this region of the empire. At around this time, Constantine began to use the title '*Victoria Gothica*' on his coins; this seems to demonstrate that he was desperate to be seen as more than the victor in a civil war, but wanted to be recognised amongst the 'good' emperors of old who expanded the empire and kept its citizens safe from the barbarian hordes to the north.[12]

After a brief interlude driving the Thaiphali from Roman-controlled lands, Constantine again spent a period of around two years touring the frontier area. This was on a far smaller scale than Hadrian's tour, of course, but it had a far more limited scope. Most of this two year period was spent with the emperor travelling between Constantinople and the Asia Minor region, mostly to Bithynia. The main purpose was probably to secure his own position as emperor; after a lengthy civil war there were bound to be disaffected members of the Roman nobility. He was also securing the frontiers and rebuilding the army after a series of devastating battles waged against his former colleagues.

For military rulers like Constantine, peaceful periods were never much more than an interlude in hostilities, and this period was no exception. In the spring of 332 Constantine was again drawn (or marched) into a conflict across the Danube. It is a common motif in Roman history for the empire to receive a 'plea for help' from a weak neighbour being threatened by a larger and stronger one. Polybius presents this as a recurring theme in Roman Republican history, and it essentially operates as a cipher; a means of justifying foreign conquest. Yet by this stage in the history of the empire, emperors were never much concerned with attempts to justify foreign expeditions, so the request may in fact be genuine.

We saw earlier that the Thaiphali had been driven into Roman territory, essentially displaced from their homelands, by the expansion of the Tervingi. At the end of 331 and into 332 this expansionist Gothic tribe were attempting to expand their territory once again. On this occasion, they were attempting to expand to the west of the territory they controlled, and into the lands of the Sarmatians. It was these Sarmatians who apparently appealed to Constantine for military aid. These Sarmatians were already well known to the Roman state, and there are claims that they were essentially a client state of Rome (that is, under Roman protection), which would explain the appeal for help and Constantine's rapid response.[13]

As an emperor and as a commander, Constantine was always thinking ahead, and in this campaign he saw an opportunity. Before setting off on the campaign he sent for his eldest surviving son, Constantine II, barely out of childhood at this time and badly lacking in any kind of military experience or military profile.[14] Constantine saw this campaign as a means of increasing his son's experience and also his standing within the military. The emperor knew that if he himself died on campaign, his son would find it almost impossible to succeed him if he was not first respected by the army.

Constantine was based in Gaul at the time and it would have taken some time for him to receive the message, gather together his field army and march east. In order to buy time, Constantine delayed the campaign for as long as he could. He did, however, move into Gothic lands, but made little effort to bring them to a pitch battle. He advanced into Moesia Secunda, close to the city of Odessos, where he made camp and awaited the arrival of his son. Constantine's intention was to allow his son to lead the invasion of Gothic territory and to build his reputation, but he would be on hand to take over if things started going wrong; a perfectly admirable strategy, but one that did require delay.

Constantine probably would have had to wait into the beginning of the winter period before his son arrived from Gaul. As soon as he arrived the campaign began in earnest. The Tervingi were campaigning to the west of the territory they controlled against the Sarmatians as noted earlier. It is a key element of this campaign that Constantine began it from the Black Sea region. To the east of the Tervingi were other groups of Sarmatians that the Tervingi were not campaigning against, but that would likely have prevented any scouts from the Tervingi warning their commanders that the Romans were massing to their rear.

The Roman campaign was rapid and decisive. They moved quickly through the lands to the east of the Sarmatian territory, and marched through relatively undefended Tervingi territory, before engaging the Tervingi army. Constantine II's victory was devastating; we hear of 100,000 barbarian casualties, either as a direct result of combat or from being driven into the wilds in wintertime.[15] It seems hardly worth saying that these casualty figures are exaggerated, but perhaps less than is usual for ancient battles statistics. This is because many civilians would have been slaughtered or driven out of their homes as the Romans marched through Tervingi lands, before they engaged the army in open combat. The 100,000 would, therefore, have been the numbers of both civilians and soldiers killed (which would, of course, push up the total number of dead, though this total is still too high and so undoubtedly exaggerated).

Constantine's victory over the Goths in the borderlands was not followed up by a more extensive campaign, one which had more decisive long term strategic aims, but was followed by peace negotiations, and then followed on quickly by a treaty. This could indicate a hidden weakness on the part of Constantine; the army had been campaigning almost continuously for many years and would have no doubt been seriously depleted following the civil war. It is likely that Constantine wanted a period of recuperation, and would have been acutely aware of the ever-present threat along his other borders. A rash foreign campaign would have been potentially disastrous for Rome at this point if it was anything less than an overwhelming success. The stakes were very high.

This defensive posture is supported by Constantine's construction of a chain of border forts along the eastern Danube frontier. These forts were not simply staging posts but serious defensive fortifications. These miniature fortresses were square in form and all had a turret at each corner: they became known as *quadriburgia* as a result.[16] The emperor was proud enough of his new constructions to celebrate their invention on coinage. This would also have been a message to the population that the emperor was acting to ensure their safety from the barbarian hoards.

It is far from clear what the terms of the treaty were, but it is likely that as a result Constantine both sent to and received gifts from the chieftains of the major Gothic tribes of the region. The treaty and this exchange of gifts had unforeseen consequences for both the Roman Empire and the barbarians from across the eastern Danube. The relative peace and stability of the border region led to a rapid and significant increase in trade, and a certain amount of exchange in cultures and ideas. Large amounts of Roman coinage flowed into the region to line the pockets of the troops stationed on the frontier who occupied the many forts. Germanic traders frequently came to the border areas without fear to sell their goods to the soldiers and trade with Roman merchants who had made the same trip. This treaty should have acted as a model for future Roman treaties: it brought peace to the constantly troubled border region of the eastern Danube for thirty years.

Whilst Constantine was securing the eastern Danube region and ultimately concluding the treaty with the Goths, a new threat was emerging on the western Danube. In order to oppose the threat to their own security, the Sarmatians had acted to arm their slaves to aid their struggles against the expanding Goths. To an extent this appears to have worked, although the Roman action against the Goths was probably more significant in diverting their attention. The policy of arming slaves may have worked in the short term, but it did not last. The Sarmatians were apparently driven from their lands by those very same slaves who saw an opportunity and made their own bid for freedom. Eusebius tells us:

> It was god himself who drove the Sarmatians under Constantine's yoke ... during a Scythian attack, they had armed their slaves in order to drive off the enemy. The slaves repelled the invaders but then turned their weapons against their masters. They drove all of them from the country.[17]

Huge numbers of displaced Sarmatians crossed the Danube with the intention of settling in Roman territory. For the final time in his life Constantine began a campaign on the Danube frontier, although much of the front line work was done by Constantine II, his eldest surviving son and natural dynastic successor. The emperor gathered together his mobile field army and marched westwards.[18] The sources preserve nothing of the content of the campaign, but the campaign likely did not consist of any great sieges or field campaigns, and was little more than the rounding up of Sarmatian settlers, with a few minor skirmishes against those who felt resistance was possible or worthwhile. All we know is the claim that 300,000 Sarmatians were rounded up and resettled within the empire in order to provide farm workers and potential new recruits to the army.[19] Eusebius tells us:

> Do I need to describe, however briefly, the way in which he subjected barbarian peoples to the authority of Rome? He was the first to subdue the Scythian and Sarmatian tribes, which never before had known servitude ... previous emperors had actually paid tribute to the Scythians ... but this would have been intolerable to Constantine.[20]

He also sums up the situation at the end of the campaign:

> The exiles could find no refuge except with Constantine; and since he was accustomed to providing sanctuary he allowed them all to

come into Roman territory. He enrolled men of military age in his
army, and to others he gave lands to provide for their needs.

These resettlements took place in a variety of locations, including Macedonia,
Thrace, Gaul and Italy.[21] This strongly implies a lack of available labour
within the empire, and potentially also a lack of military recruits, hence
Constantine's desire to make good use of these men. The exact dates of the
campaign are unknown, but the emperor is recorded present at Singidunum
(modern Belgrade) on 5 July 334 and at Naissus on 25 August.[22] Singidunum
is on the Danube, but Naissus is some way to the south. The campaign
we can therefore infer, peaked on or around the beginning of July and
Constantine moved south after its successful conclusion.

After gaining the western empire, defeating his eastern counterpart
and securing the Danube frontier, in Constantine's eyes only one enemy
remained: the Persian Shah, Shapur II. Constantine was aging and perhaps
did not have the powers he had once possessed, but this did not stop him
from wishing to extend the boundaries of the Christian empire eastwards.

This gradual eastwards movement is something that Constantine does
appear to have had in his mind for some time before 334. Records of
speeches that have survived suggest that he had imagined such an eastwards
movement since the very start of his career.[23] How early Constantine planned
the eastern campaign is open to speculation, but I suspect that the planning
was quite late; the aspiration however may have been considerably earlier.

Shortly after defeating Licinius, Constantine received emissaries from
Shapur. We do not know what message these emissaries brought, but the fact
that they were sent is entirely understandable. To look from the perspective
of Shapur and the Persians: he had had a relatively peaceful western border
whilst Licinius was in power, but with the coming of the civil war on his
most dangerous border, and his old neighbour's defeat, Shapur would have
wished to reassert the relative peace with his new neighbour and between his
empire and that of Rome.

The response Shapur received was perhaps not as positive as he would
have liked. Constantine replied with a very lengthy excursus on his new
religious faith. He restated his military successes over the persecutors of
Christians, and his desire to see Shapur protect Christians within the Persian
Empire from persecution by any members of other faiths.[24] It is far from
clear whether or not Shapur was treating Christians poorly in the east, and
this may simply have been an example of Constantine's realpolitik disguised
in the terms of religion and ethics: perhaps he was making a political point to
his new neighbour and attempting to assert a measure of dominance right
from their first encounter.

At around the time Constantine was resettling the Sarmatians, Shapur removed from power the Christian king of Armenia, and replaced him with a candidate who had a more Persian-centred view. The Persians had lost control of the Armenia region to Galerius in 298, and they had wanted to reassert their control ever since.[25] Whilst Constantine was engaged on the Danube frontier, Shapur took his opportunity to seize control of Armenia. This was an ambitious move that was bound to cause conflict with Rome, and in hindsight Shapur had perhaps left his move too late. Constantine was completing his conquests and his attention was turning east; if Shapur had made his move shortly after Constantine's defeat of Licinius, he may have had more opportunity to consolidate his new gain before being challenged.

Constantine counter-moved by sending his son, Constantine II, to the east at the head of a large force. It is interesting that Constantine did not himself immediately move to the region; he was quite elderly by this time and aware of his own frailty. He was also evidently considering the succession and the need to expose his chosen successor to a difficult military and political crisis in order that he may prove his worth.

Constantine II's first response to the crisis was not military, but diplomatic. There are several reasons for this. The most important of these is that Constantine evidently did intend to lead the troops himself, but as yet was not present on the eastern front, perhaps resting after a tiring Danubian campaign, or perhaps gathering more troops. Either way, military action was delayed.

Constantine II's attempts at negotiations with Shapur, which began in 335, did not last long and were an abject failure. The Persians were in no mood to negotiate, and in all likelihood the negotiations were a ploy to buy time on the part of the Romans whilst they awaited the arrival of the emperor in person. In 336 Constantine received a second delegation from the Persian Emperor; the contents of the negotiations are unknown but it is reasonable to speculate that Shapur would have attempted to reassert the terms of the previously peaceful relations with Rome, though with Armenia remaining under his control. This was, of course, unacceptable to Constantine and the ambassadors were dismissed swiftly.

In 337 Constantine moved into Asia Minor where he personally supervised the gathering together of the *comitatenses* and made the final preparations for war with Persia. However, whilst at Nicomedia he fell gravely ill and was quickly moved to the Achyron Villa. Constantine, the first Christian emperor, died there on 22 May 337.[26] His body was carried to Constantinople by his son, Constantine II, where it was interred.

Constantine's decision to go to war with Shapur plunged the Roman Empire into a generation of warfare on the eastern front. If he had accepted the terms offered by Shapur this could perhaps have been avoided. This is easy to suggest with hindsight, however, and in all likelihood the Persians would have taken Constantine's death as a signal to invade, treaty or no.

The truth of his life was this: Constantine had succeeded in uniting the empire once again under a strong single ruler, but had relinquished some of that power by appointing others to the role of Caesar and Augustus (although whilst he was alive there was never a doubt who the real power in the empire was). He secured the western empire and the Danubian border and brought religious and political stability to most of the empire while he reigned. Whatever his successes and failures, the empire was never quite the same again.

Chapter 10

The Future of the Roman Empire

Constantine's life and rule mark a watershed in the history and trans-formation of the Roman Empire. While it is important not to exaggerate or overstate this, it is certainly clear that Constantine's patronage, his leverage, his interpretation of his own role both as Christian and emperor, and thus the development of the way power worked in the Roman Empire, were key to its subsequent history.

When Constantine died in 337 he left behind him an empire centred now around Constantinople and which was on the road to transformation, in no small part due to his influence and actions, to become the Byzantine Empire of later centuries that helped sustain European culture and letters while the western empire (even including Rome, which fell to the barbarians early in the fifth century) variously suffered from internal discord and external invasion. Constantine's long and successful imperial career as patron, promoter and protector of the Christian faith had lasted around twenty-five years. In this time, he had achieved much and in many arenas; so much so that it may have seemed difficult for his contemporaries to imagine another of his kind. In keeping with a life lived very much on the public and political stage, his funeral rites were a public and extravagant affair. Eusebius tells us about them as follows:

> The military took up the remains and laid them in a golden coffin. They wrapped this in imperial purple, and bore it into the city named after the Emperor; then in the most superb of all the imperial halls they laid it on a high pedestal, and by kindling lights all round on golden stands they provided a wonderful spectacle for the onlookers of a kind never seen on earth by anyone under the light of the sun from the first creation of the world. Within the palace itself, in the central imperial quarters, the Emperor's remains,

adorned with imperial ornaments, with purple and crown, was guarded day and night by a huge circle of people keeping vigil.[1]

Not only were Constantine's funeral rites spectacular (as had been his military victories, his religious building programme, his patronage of Christianity, his move of the Roman imperial capital from its ancestral home to a city refashioned in his honour and named for him) but they were also entirely in line with the now Christianised ways of thinking about the emperor as divinely instituted, and thus in his turn heavily responsible to God. Eusebius again:

> The commanders of the whole army, the *comites* and all the ruling class, who were bound by law to pay homage to the Emperor first, making no change in their usual routine, filed past at the required times and saluted the Emperor on the bier with genuflections after his death in the same way as when he was alive. After these chief persons the members of the Senate and all those of official rank came and did the same, and after them crowds of people of all classes with their wives and children came to look. These proceedings continued for a long time, the military having decided that the remains should stay there and be watched until his sons should arrive and pay respects to their father by personally attending to the rites. Alone of mortals the Blessed One reigned even after death, and the customs were maintained just as if he were alive, God having granted this to him and no other since time began. Alone therefore among Emperors and unlike any other he had honoured by acts of every kind the all-sovereign God and his Christ, and it is right that he alone enjoyed these things, as the God over all allowed his mortal part to reign among mankind, thus demonstrating the ageless and deathless reign of his soul to those with minds not stony-hard.[2]

In looking at the manner of Constantine's funeral rites so closely, what become apparent are the keys to understanding what happened to the Roman Empire after Constantine. Firstly, there is the lavish attention to detail, the pomp, the grandeur and the ceremony which combined elements both of the traditional pagan and the new Christian. Secondly, there is the new power dynamic at work, a new Christian ceremonial: the Christian God, it was now thought, uniquely favoured Constantine over all others; how else could one man have achieved so much and gone so far, but by divine favour? Such religious favouritism, as compared against the spiritually egalitarian trend to be found in New Testament ethics that partly helps explain the immediate appeal of Christianity to out-groups, makes it clear that Christianity and Roman imperial power, by means of their intersection in the person of Constantine and as a consequence of his military victory, had both become something different. They had both been transformed.

The problems of inheritance

Although Constantine's funeral as described by Eusebius was carried out with all due ceremony, respect and homage, and in all likelihood gave the impression to the onlookers of all that was the best in smooth Roman state operations, it in fact masked a more troubling and confusing reality. And the reality was the problem of succession. Constantine had been a man unique and an emperor apart; on his death, it was not entirely clear who could or would step into his shoes. In fact, this problem was largely created by Constantine himself. Constantine being the good emperor and decisive man of action that he was, had naturally taken the time to think about what would happen to the Roman Empire after his death before he died. His plans for succession were actually a little on the complicated side. In an effort to be fair to his many heirs and extended family, he had actually factored in not only his three remaining sons, but also his relatives through his step-mother Theodora. Potential candidates for the imperial title from both of these sets of families had been given honours (such as being made Caesar) or the hand in marriage of a high-ranking female family member (such as Constantina, the daughter of Constantine) and this had all happened in the immediate years before Constantine's death. However, such dissolute power structures did not sit well with the demands of the Roman Empire at the time of Constantine's death: the nature of the position and role of emperor always did require one man to fill it. From the history of Constantine's military career itself, we already know how shaky and infirm any attempts at power-sharing, as in the Tetrarchy that preceded him, could turn out to be.

Indeed, so confused and troubled was this reality post-Constantine that the post of emperor was a position vacant for over three months. It was finally filled by all three of his surviving sons: Constantine II, Constantius II and Constans were all officially recognised as Augusti. But the gap of over three months masked yet another troubling reality: it took such a long time for the power vacuum that had opened up at the heart of the Roman Empire to be filled because that time was needed by Constantine's troops, with the likely involvement of at least one of his sons (Constantius II, who was actually present in Constantinople around the time his father died), to get rid of any potential threats and challenges from Theodora's side of the family. In that period, nine members from Theodora's branch were killed brutally. Indeed, of this side of the family, only two were left alive: Julian and his half-brother Gallus. The former was only a young boy at the time of the swift extermination of most of the rest of his male relatives, but was to grow up to become the apostate emperor Julian (defiantly and eccentrically pagan) with a colourful, albeit fairly brief, rule. And so once these threats were all eliminated, Constantine's troops were happy to swear allegiance to the only men they could view as the rightful heirs of Constantine: his sons.

However, the bloody political intrigue was not quite yet over. As the state history of the Roman Empire so often demonstrates, power-sharing, and especially between family members, was not often a triumphant success of co-operation, harmony and mutual accord. Constantine's three sons, now all vying for supremacy, rank and authority, were bound to start the in-fighting that would eventually eliminate two of them, leaving one coming out on top as emperor. This process was set in motion when the sons all met in Pannonia and divided up the empire between them, as follows:

- To Constantine II, the eldest brother, the western provinces of Gaul, Spain and Britain.
- To Constantius II, the east and Thrace.
- To Constans, Moesia, Illyricum, Italy and Africa.

While this might seem as if an equitable power-sharing arrangement had established itself on firm foundations, with the empire divided up according to geographical and regional loyalties, in reality it was nothing of the sort. With the Roman Empire divided into three parts, the three sons were left unsatisfied in the sense that none of them could feel himself to be sole ruler and all-powerful in the way that their father Constantine had been. However, there were more pressing matters at hand: various external threats to the security of the Roman Empire were making themselves felt and the sons were needed on the field of battle, to honour their father's memory in this regard as he would no doubt have wanted. While the sons were away doing this, the internal discords and the unsatisfactory power-sharing arrangements started to show signs of fracture. The oldest son, Constantine II, since he was the senior of the three, naturally also thought of himself as the superior, and thus the sole and rightful heir of Constantine and emperor of the Roman Empire. To this end, he had started making moves to assert his own position and authority over his brothers and their territory, in particular over the younger Constans.

This discord came to a head in 340, when Constantine II took his troops into northern Italy, Constans' own territory. Although Constans himself was not there in person to lead his troops against his brother's invasion, Constantine II's forces were met by Constans' own. It turned out that Constantine II's upstart ambitions were his downfall; his troops were taken completely by surprise and, very much hoisted by his own petard, he was himself killed. This swift and decisive end to Constantine II's attempts to assume full power left Constans in a strong position indeed. With no one now in charge of Constantine II's share of the Roman Empire, Constans was free to invade and take as much of the west as he could. This he did, leaving the middle brother, Constantius II, still heavily involved in his own troubles in the east, where he was fighting the Persians and so unable and unwilling to take advantage of the power vacuum and territorial disputes that had been created on Constantine II's demise.

Constans settled into the demands of ruling his new and expanded territory with ease; the memory of Constantine II did not seem to trouble either him or his new subjects over much, since there was no uprising, no revolt, and no hostility of great note to be found among the peoples of the west who now abruptly found themselves with a new man in charge. In fact, the inherent tensions built into the concept of power-sharing seemed to have gone away, at least for the meantime; Constans stayed within his territory and ruled for most of the rest of the 340s, while Constantius II remained in his. This seemed a happy enough arrangement; as had happened before, the Roman Empire was divided more or less along east/west lines and the two remaining brothers were satisfied with this.

Christianity, power and the army

But the fault lines were there, nonetheless: both Christianity and the nature of power in the Roman Empire were transformed by their mutual intersection. The sons of Constantine embodied the new stage in the transformation that was being played out: whereas Constantine had come to the faith in his adult years, as a soldier who felt he owed his great success to the Christian God, and only later developing his understanding of his faith with the benefit of the new Christian discourse that he came into contact with, his son Constans had already been baptized a Christian. The implication of this being that Constans, right from the first day he assumed power, was ruling both as a Christian but also as the Roman emperor: this had not happened before, and the difference it made to the nature of power in the Roman empire and to what it meant to be Roman emperor, was immense. Most importantly of all, it threw up a very new question: what did it mean to be both a man of war (as the Roman emperor must inevitably be) *and* a man of God? The answer was, of course, not easy or obvious because the question had never before been asked in quite this way. Thus, Constantine and his successors were part of the formulation of that answer: how to combine a faith that could have a distinctly pacifist interpretation with that of a more pragmatic military reality. One answer to that question is to look to Constantine's successors: Constans, took his own role as protector and defender of the faith just as seriously as his father had.

Nevertheless, Constans was also a pragmatist, like his father, and he did not enact tough legislation of a kind to make traditional Greco-Roman paganism illegal or impermissible overnight. As an example of his legislative agenda, in 341 he condemned pagan cult worship, specifically the practice of animal sacrifice.[3] This is the first example of a condemnation of this kind; Constantine's own anti-pagan legislation already came with a precedent of its own. We can see the pragmatism at work: animal sacrifice is condemned, but there is not much detailing the punishments or consequences to those found practising it. In other words, Constans here is charting a difficult course between needing to satisfy the demands coming from the Christian intelligentsia to stamp out pagan practice, and those of contemporary pagans, many of whom were prominent, powerful and unlikely to take kindly to outright hostility.

Not only was a new Christian culture being forged in the books and statutes of Roman law, but also in the councils and meetings of bishops and clergy. Here, yet more transformation was taking place, building on the events set in motion by Constantine himself. The North African schism and Constantine's involvement in what started as essentially an ecclesiastical breakdown of relations showed how intertwined church and state were becoming, though all the while still establishing for themselves separate identities in the new Christian context. Constantine's sincere desire to make harmony and unity out of discord established the precedent for secular involvement in church disputes, even ones based on technicalities, inter-pretation and doctrinal wrangling: the more natural happy hunting ground of theologians rather than emperors. Constans picked up his father's baton and ran: just like his father before him, he too was confronted with a church beset by conflicting forces, being torn apart by competing interests and endlessly good at creating doctrinal discord. And just like his father, perhaps even more so given the fact that he had always been a Christian as an emperor, he felt keenly his sense of duty towards God and his religious responsibility as emperor.

If we see these fault lines appearing in what it meant to be a Roman emperor in the measured legislative decisions of Constans and in the involvement of secular power (Constantine) in doctrinal disputes, then this is no less the case when we turn to consider Christianity in the Roman army.

Besides having an egalitarian interpretation which made it attractive to marginalised groups, as already discussed, the other distinctly problematic thing about Christianity was its marked pacifism.[4] Surprisingly enough, this still presented no problem to its success as a religion in the decidedly non-pacifist Roman state: during the fourth century, Christianity and the military certainly came into contact, albeit slowly, though to my mind this was not due to any particular ideological clash. Rather, army recruitment was happening at the frontiers or non-urban regions, and these were the very same places where Christianity was least in evidence, and found it hardest to access, given that in the first three centuries of its life Christianity was overwhelmingly urban.

In terms of direct missionary activity among the army, it certainly appears that Constantine himself was responsible for some of this, though on a very small-scale: fellow Christians in the army were given Sundays off, for example, as Eusebius reports:

> He also decreed that the truly sovereign and really first day, the day of the Lord and Saviour, should be considered a regular day of prayer. Servants and ministers consecrated to God, men whose well-ordered life was marked by reverent conduct and every virtue, were put in charge of the whole household, and faithful praetorians, bodyguards armed with the practice of faithful loyalty, adopted the Emperor as their tutor in religious conduct, themselves paying no less honour to the Lord's saving day and on it joining in the prayers the Emperor loved.[5]

Though other historians have argued that in Constantine's day, perhaps as many as 'two thirds of his government at the top were non-Christian.'[6] Further on, though still to be read with some moderation, given Eusebius' tendency to eulogise Constantine:

> The Day of Salvation then, which also bears the names of Light Day and Sun Day, he taught all the military to revere devoutly. To those who shared the divinely given faith he allowed free time to attend unhindered the church of God, on the assumption that with all impediment removed they would join in the prayers.[7]

Evidently, Constantine himself saw no difficulty between his new-found faith and its potentially pacifist interpretation, and his emperorship (else conversion would have necessitated stepping down from office) and neither did he expect the same issue to apply to those in his service, since it seems here that being a soldier and being a Christian are not conceptualised as mutually exclusive. That Christianity did not deter male converts from also bearing arms reminds us that Christianity was fitting into existing power structures just as much as it was also changing them. The result of this was neither the disbanding of the army nor the death of Christianity, but rather a blend of the military reality and the new religion: a form of military Christianity arose over time; the image being that of a Christian soldier, one who was fighting for Christ. Christian soldiers who killed in battle only had to do penance afterwards, but apart from that by the fifth century at the latest, being a Christian and having a professional army career presented no conceptual or ideological challenge.[8]

Constantine's religious building programme

To demonstrate this, we have Constantine's enduring religious building programme as evidence of a new Christian culture. For example, in Rome from 312–313 Constantine created many rich basilicas for the church, and these are the more famed of Constantine's religious building programme. However, also of note are those built in cities such as Constantinople itself, Trier, Antioch, Nicomedia and Jerusalem.[9] Besides creating a material culture which would make Christianity appear as the favoured religion it now was, Constantine also helped the church by handing over gifts of land and other forms of wealth to these new basilicas, thus helping the church on the road to becoming a significant power broker in its own right in the later Roman Empire.

These actions of Constantine's, besides pointing to his own self-image and identity as a man of action and emperor, also indicate that Constantine was starting to work out more carefully what his own role would be within the faith. Constantine was not to be a leading light on the stage of Christian theology, though he held those kinds of men who were (such as Lactantius) in high regard. He did himself take pains to read the Bible, talk and discuss points of doctrine with Lactantius and other scholars, and to work out a new and satisfying intellectual paradigm for himself in which he could place his new faith. Given how thoroughly drenched he and his fellow Romans were in the traditional paganism of the Roman Empire of his time, this was no mean feat, and naturally attracted the brightest and best minds who enjoyed working through these complications and then transmitting their thinking to men such as Constantine. And men such as Constantine, once they had started towards making for themselves a new intellectual culture, naturally saw themselves as protectors or guardians of the new faith.

Constantine's legislative programme

In order to further cement the new power of the church, Constantine also created favourable legislation. For example, church land was exempted from being taxed; provincial officials were ordered to provide labour and materials for church construction where available; a system of giving food gifts to churches was put in place and also gifts of grain rations were handed out to church poor (such as widows) and to others who were in the service of the church; church clerics were exempted from taking on the burden of excessive state/secular obligations and Constantine ensured that these clerics were provided for with regular contributions from the public purse. All in all, Constantine generously provided the church with the structures, systems and frameworks it needed to become a fully-functioning and powerful institution in its own right. The effect of all this incredible state patronage, wealth and power was to change the social demographic of Christianity. This did not happen immediately, but it should be easy enough to understand how attractive a clerical position, which also came with the distinct advantage of being exempted from tiresome civic duties, costs and responsibilities, would seem to ambitious and literate men for whom a career in the army or civil service was either not feasible or not all that appealing. In other words, Constantine's other enduring legacy was to start the process of establishing the favourable conditions that were necessary to attract the men who had power, education and prestige.

Besides actively legislating for Christianity, Constantine also enacted laws whose ultimate effect was to suppress or curtail the traditions of Greco-Roman paganism. Although Constantine did not engage in a vast persecution agenda, as previous emperors had against early Christianity, he was not averse to anti-pagan legislation of his own. For example, he ordered that all eunuch-priests in Egypt be 'exterminated' since they were considered aberrations and transgressions of the divine order; he also decreed that the practise of making eunuchs should itself be forbidden henceforth. Moreover, Constantine banned cult acts that were performed to tell the future. While it was not the case that either of these items of legislation was entirely new or without precedent (eunuch-making and fortune-telling were both features of the broad church of Greco-Roman paganism that had fallen foul of official-dom before: eunuch-making on humane grounds and fortune telling on the grounds of state security; perhaps a version of ancient counter-terrorism), neither should it be overlooked that Constantine's stated aims at the start of his reign were for religious toleration, it still seems that this kind of legislation was a strike at the old ways. Although paganism was hardly persecuted in any large-scale way under Constantine's rule, the process of curtailment, the erosion of the power invested in paganism and of its characteristic and distinctive features was certainly set in motion and followed through by Constans.

To the fourth century, and beyond

Moving away from the meeting of Christianity and the military, Constantine and the reworking of power that was underway, the remainder of the significant military events of the fourth century deserve a broader overview here before making some concluding remarks on Constantine's military career and successes as an emperor.

From 354 onwards, our best primary source for telling the events of the next half of the third century, and for giving us our base knowledge of how the Roman army actually functioned, is Ammianus Marcellinus. Although his name is not as widely known as that of the great Roman historians such as Tacitus or Livy, he ranks among them for his historical achievement and for being, to many, the last of the great Roman historians. What is particularly interesting about Ammianus is that he was not a professional historian; in fact, he was a soldier and, unusually, was actually contemporary to the events he described and analysed. As a pagan, he must also receive much credit for his fair-handed treatment of Christianity and his general absence of single-minded rhetorical aims and biases. Finally, he set himself the immense task of picking up where Tacitus had left off; the Tacitean history finishes in 96, and Ammianus wrote the history of events after that date until his own time. It is most unfortunate indeed that much of his work is now lost; what does remain only covers the years 354–378. However, it is fortunate that his work on this period does survive; without it, it would be a much harder task to reconstruct the reigns of Constantius, Gallus, Julian, Jovian, Valentinian and Valens.

Besides Ammianus, we also have the historian Procopius of Caesarea. Like Ammianus, Procopius also knew military service (fighting for Belisarius, in places such as Italy, Persia and Africa), but he lived after Ammianus, in the sixth century. Also like Ammianus, he was writing in the genre of literary narrative history, and so, in contrast to the author Vegetius, both authors have a less accurate use of technical vocabulary and discussion of the real practicalities. Thus Vegetius can work to complement Ammianus and Procopius; the former is not in the genre of narrative but is rather a treatise on the 'science' of war; the latter two narrative historians who are successful for having personal, first-hand experience of what it is to be on the field of battle.

It is easy to see why 350 can be considered a turning-point. In this year, Constans was assassinated, making him the second of Constantine's heirs to find his death to be one of the problems of inheritance. This left only

Constantius II as sole heir and emperor, but the ghost of the Tetrarchy must have haunted him, because he made Gallus (one of the two young male members of the imperial family to survive the bloodletting in the months following Constantine's death) Caesar and gave him the control over the east in his place. He did this for a good reason, though: he was required to march out against Magnentius, a usurper who had seized Constans' power after his death. Constantius II's campaign against Magnentius was sustained: he took until 353 to finally bring back the empire to him; to reconquer the west. It is from this point that Ammianus' history, as it survives, starts.

Although Gallus had some military and strategic successes in ruling the east (according to Ammianus, he waged a successful campaign against the Persians), he is generally considered a bad emperor. He, along with his wife Constantina (the same daughter of Constantine) gained for themselves a reputation for brutality and cruelty in their managing of public affairs. However, fortunately for cities such as Antioch which experienced this first hand, Gallus' reign in the purple was short-lived. He was executed in late 354, charged with having brought about the deaths of representatives of Constantius II. This latter must have considered whether his experiment in power-sharing was worth continuing; the idea remained with him, because in 355 he engaged Julian (the other surviving half-brother) in a power-sharing agreement. Julian was offered the hand of Helena, another daughter of Constantine's and thus a sister of Constantius II, to cement his role in the imperial family and Constantius II's favour. Julian proved his military mettle in his first campaign, in 356, to win back Gaul; thus Constantius II and Julian were clearly in partnership at this time.

However, Julian was something of a black sheep in the family, and in many ways, the most interesting and unusual emperor produced by the fourth century after Constantine himself. He became emperor in his own right in 361, on the death of Constantius II, and by this time had thoroughly fleshed out for himself his own world-view and self-image: he was defiantly and intellectually a pagan. He saw himself as standing against the new religion that Constantine had helped to usher in, and moreover, was confident that the old gods would help him on the road to overthrowing Christianity. It is another one of those interesting historical games to speculate what would have happened had Julian's reign lasted longer than the two years that it did; the emperor died in June 363 on the battlefield. In typical style for a man who had made a name for being somewhat eccentric in his paganism, unhappily lacking in the important ability to not regularly infuriate and annoy those about him (crucially, his army included), and devoted to extravagant animal sacrifice to honour the gods, his death was rash and sudden. He ran out of his tent to summon the rest of the Roman troops after his column was attacked at the rear on their way to Samarra. He made the fatal mistake of doing this without first putting on his full armour: in the melee he was one of the casualties, killed by a spear. So ended the short, but colourful, life of Julian; Ammianus, himself a fellow pagan and supporter of Julian, shows his regard for the man by devoting roughly half of his history to his reign alone.

The emperor Jovian is the next in line; with him ends the direct link to the family of Constantine (at least both Gallus and Julian had been married to daughters of Constantine). Unlike those who had gone before, Jovian's only claim to fame was that in 361 he had gone with the body of Constantius II as it was taken back to Constantinople for burial. However, the Roman army were in dire straits with the sudden and unexpected death of Julian, and all were aware of the need for someone to take charge, and soon. Since the senior military men were unable to make a successful decision regarding who that should be, it fell to a few among the rank and file to seize on Jovian and to proclaim him emperor. There were no other candidates at this point that seemed satisfactory, so Jovian was probably just the least-worst option. However, if Julian's rule was to prove short-lived, then the same is true even more so of Jovian; in early 364 he was found dead in his room under suspicious circumstances. Although his death was passed off as accidental, Ammianus suggests to us that in fact he was strangled.

After Jovian came more struggles for succession in the form of Valentinian and his brother Valens. Valentinian was the candidate of choice, but out of a sense of family responsibility he elected to share power with his brother who was not as senior as him.

The Battle of Adrianople: the fall of Rome; the rise of Byzantium

Although the reign of Valens and Valentinian was marked by some military success, it is the defining Battle of Adrianople in 378 for which Valens in particular is remembered. This is a good place to mark the end of the history of Constantine's successors and the future of the Roman Empire, because it was such an unexpectedly crushing defeat: the worst that Rome had suffered since the dark days of the Battle of Cannae at the hands of Hannibal in 216 BC, in the eyes of its historian, Ammianus. Needless to say, the Battle of Adrianople stands in marked contrast to Constantine's own military successes.

In 378, Valens had moved from Antioch to Constantinople, and reports were received to indicate that there were substantial numbers of Goths massing around Adrianople. The pressure was on and Valens could not put off any longer dealing with this substantial threat; he marched his army to Adrianople, but was waiting for the western army, under the western emperor Gratian, to join him so they could fight with their combined forces. However, Valens was keen to win glory in what he thought would be a fairly easy victory, and moreover to take back the strategically important Danube region from Gothic control. He was thus not inclined to wait for Gratian and thus miss out on winning such honour; his major strategic and tactical mistake was to engage the enemy too soon, and also, to refuse to make negotiations with the Goths over Thrace, who at this point would have been appeased had they been ceded this territory, and mostly desiring to avoid a war themselves. It was after making these two major errors that Valens decided to commence battle in August, on a plain outside the city of Adrianople and in the direction of the Gothic encampment. 'At about two o'clock in the afternoon the legionaries caught sight of the wagons of the Goths, drawn into a huge circle around the perimeter of their camp, and the Goths lit fires in the already hot sun, while their leaders stalled for time. However, the Battle of Adrianople did not start with precision timing; rather, there was an unexpected outbreak of violence between some sections of the Romans and Goths. Two Goth commanders caught sight of this first engagement, and they led their men right into the Roman ranks.

This first clash was also brutal: the Roman left-wing pushed ahead and were within striking distance of the Gothic encampment, but they lost the vital support of the cavalry and so were ultimately unsuccessful. Then the Romans had bitter hand-to-hand fighting to contend with, and missiles which landed on the ranks without mercy. In the baking dusty heat, the Roman army were naturally worn down: Valens had not given them the benefit that a delay (with full rest and reinvigoration) would have afforded; it was hot, they had marched long just days before and they had been in line and fighting since the break of day. In this dire situation, Valens tried in vain to incite his troops and encourage them on, but the Romans could no longer take such a hammering. The unthinkable had actually happened: the Goths were succeeding in punching a hole through the unbreakable line of the Roman army; men, units and the Roman military order and disciple that was the key to its success were being torn to shreds right before everyone's eyes. The Romans that did remain started to flee the field of battle; Valens could not find his back-up troops; the Goths knew the victory was theirs for the taking and did not give up at this late stage.

The defeat was total and bloody; less than a third of Valens' army escaped with their lives, and modern historians estimate that somewhere in the region of 15,000 to 30,000 Roman soldiers died, including many high-ranking members. Though Valens escaped the greater part of the onslaught, he was himself killed by an arrow. His body was never recovered from the mess, which left the way clear for legend and story to explain what had actually happened to him.[10]

What a contrast the life of Valens, just a few decades after that of Constantine. Whereas the latter had military know-how, strategy and good fortune all on his side, the former goes down in history as the man responsible for this humiliating and catastrophic Roman defeat. After the death of Valens, a power vacuum again opened up in the affairs of the Roman state, but this time there was not a man of Constantine's calibre, capable of taking on the responsibility of the Roman state and turning unpromising and chaotic circumstances into victory and order, as he had done.

It is fitting to leave the final word to Ammianus, who relates this most crushing of Roman defeats as follows:

> Amid the clashing of arms and weapons on every side, while Bellona, raging with more than her usual fury, was sounding the death-knell of the Roman cause, our retreating troops rallied with shouts of mutual encouragement. But, as the fighting spread like fire and numbers of them were transfixed by arrows and whirling javelins, they lost heart. Then the opposing lines came into collision like ships of war and pushed each other to and fro, heaving under the reciprocal motion like the waves of the sea. Our left wing penetrated as far as the very wagons, and would have gone further if it had received any support, but it was abandoned by the rest of the cavalry, and under pressure of numbers gave way and collapsed like a broken dyke. This left the infantry unprotected and so closely huddled together that a man could hardly wield his sword or draw back his arm once he had stretched it out. Dust rose in such clouds as to hide the sky, which rang with frightful shouts. In consequence it was impossible to see the enemy's missiles in flight and dodge them; all found their mark and dealt death on every side. The barbarians poured on in huge columns, trampling down horse and man and crushing our ranks so as to make an orderly retreat impossible. Our men were too close-packed to have any hope of escape; so they resolved to die like heroes, faced the enemy's swords, and struck back at their assailants. On both sides helmets and breast-plates were split in pieces by blows from the battle-axe. You might see a lion-hearted savage, who had been hamstrung or had lost his right hand or been wounded in the side, grinding his clenched teeth and casting defiant glances around in the very throes of death. In this mutual slaughter so many were laid low that the field was covered with the bodies of

the slain, while the groans of the dying and severely wounded filled all who heard them with abject fear.

In this scene of total confusion the infantry, worn out by toil and danger, had no strength or sense left to form a plan. Most had had their spears shattered in the constant collisions, so they made do with their drawn swords and plunged into the dense masses of the foe, regardless of their lives and aware that there was no hope of escape. The ground was so drenched with blood that they slipped and fell, but they strained every nerve to sell their lives dearly, and faced their opponents with such resolution that some perished at the hands of their own comrades. In the end, when the whole field was one dark pool of blood and they could see nothing but heaps of slain wherever they turned their eyes, they tramped without scruple on the lifeless corpses.

The sun, which was high in the sky (it was moving into the house of the Virgin after traversing Leo) scorched the Romans, who were weak from hunger, parched with thirst, and weighted down by the burden of their armour. Finally, our line gave way under the overpowering pressure of the barbarians, and as a last resort our men took to their heels in a general sauve qui peut.

While all were scattering in flight over unfamiliar paths, the emperor [Valens] was in a situation of frightful peril. He picked his way slowly over the heaps of bodies and took refuge with the Lancearii and Mattiarii, who stood firm and unshaken as long as they could withstand the pressure of superior numbers. His bodyguard had left him, and when Trajan saw him he cried out that all was lost unless he could be protected by the foreign auxiliaries. At this count Victor rushed off to bring up the Batavi to the emperor's assistance. They had been placed in reserve not far off, but not one of them was to be found. So Victor retired and left the field. Richomer and Saturninus saved themselves in the same way.

The barbarians' eyes flashed fire as they pursued their dazed foe, whose blood ran cold with terror. Some fell without knowing who struck them, some were crushed by sheer weight of numbers, and some were killed by their own comrades. They could neither gain ground by resistance nor obtain mercy by giving way. Besides, many lay blocking the way half dead, unable to endure the agony of their wounds, and the carcasses of slaughtered horses covered the ground in heaps. At last a moonless night brought an end to these irreparable losses, which cost Rome so dear.

Soon after nightfall, so it was supposed, the emperor was mortally wounded by an arrow and died immediately. No one admitted that he had seen him or been near him, and it was presumed that he fell among common soldiers, but his body was never found.[11]

Chapter 11

Constantinople: War and the City

Well after Constantine's own time, Constantinople gloried in its reputation for being a city that was near-impossible for any invading foreign force to capture. This, the removal of the imperial capital to the east, besides Constantine's Christian legacy built on the back of his military success, was the second of his major achievements.

But how difficult was it for the citizenry of the Roman empire to stomach this change of capital? Emperors had not lived in Rome, and had only been occasional visitors, for more than a generation and this certainly helped to downgrade its status. Rome was also no longer of great strategic importance because the conflict areas had changed. The threats to the frontiers of the Rhine, Danube and the east meant that cities closer to those regions were typically the seat of emperors. For this reason, Constantine spent a great deal of time in Trier, for example, before the civil war. Nevertheless, practically speaking, Constantinople was superior to Rome in several key ways:

- It was strategically well sited, being the gateway not only from east to west, but north to south.
- It controlled the grain trade out of the Black Sea and whoever controlled the city could, therefore, control that trade (although the Black Sea region was not the only exporter of grain of course).
- It occupied a very defensible location. It was true that the city had only fallen after a siege to two emperors: Septimius Severus (only after a difficult siege) and Constantine himself. Once the city had been properly fortified it became a stronghold far exceeding the defensive capabilities of Rome.
- Constantinople could also be supplied by sea. As long as the city maintained naval supremacy in its waters, it could not be starved into submission and could receive regular reinforcements and resupplies as required. In comparison, Rome had to be supplied from a port at

Ostia some miles away from the city which had all the potential difficulties of interruptions to the lines of supply as were faced by Athens and its port at Piraeus.

Indeed, for all these reasons, this was why the fall of Constantinople in 1453 came as such a severe shock to its citizenry, who had become accustomed to thinking that they were untouchable behind their strong city walls, invulnerable until only the end of days itself came. This strong belief in the impregnability of their own city is yet another legacy for which later Constantinopolitans have to thank Constantine. Making the city strong, defensive and well-guarded against foreign attack (the sack of the city in 1204 by a 'friendly' fourth crusade notwithstanding) was part of Constantine's plan to build an imperial city worthy of the name, and as a man well-versed in military strategy and necessity, he was not a man to overlook the importance of city defence. We learn more about Constantine's building programme of improvements from the Easter Chronicle:

> In the time of the aforementioned consuls, Constantine the celebrated emperor departed from Rome and, while staying at Nicomedia metropolis of Bithynia, made visitations for a long time to Byzantium. He renewed the first wall of the city of Byzas, and after making considerable extensions also to the same wall he joined them to the ancient wall of the city and named it Constantinople; he also completed the Hippodrome, adorning it with works in bronze and with every excellence, and made in it a box for imperial viewing in likeness of the one which is in Rome.[1]

According to the same source, Constantine also made a palace for the new city and a forum with the famous column at the centre with the statue of himself at the top; another clear mark of Constantine's imperial designs for the city to rival and even surpass Rome herself. However, not all sources are pro-Constantine in their evaluation of his civic strategy and building programme. The anti-Constantine Zosimus tells us that Constantine's decisions regarding city defence were poor in comparison to his predecessor Diocletian, and that he made a tactical error in removing armies from the frontiers (where they were needed) to the cities (where they were not, and where they had the ability to do a great deal of damage):

> Constantine did something else which gave the barbarians un-hindered access to the Roman Empire. By the forethought of Diocletian, the frontiers of the empire everywhere were covered, as I have stated, with cities, garrisons and fortifications which housed the whole army. Consequently it was impossible for the

barbarians to cross the frontier because they were confronted at every point by forces capable of resisting their attacks. Constantine destroyed this security by removing most of the troops from the frontiers and stationing them in cities which did not need assistance, thus both stripping of protection those being molested by the barbarians and subjecting the cities left alone by them to the outrages of the soldiers, so that henceforth most have become deserted. Moreover he enervated the troops by allowing them to devote themselves to shows and luxuries. In plain terms, Constantine was the origin and beginning of the present destruction of the empire.[2]

Zosimus' accusations here of imperial incompetence and poor military strategy need to be examined further; particularly so since other references would suggest that Constantine was very far from being a poor decision maker, and since other references have been painting for us a portrait of a man who knew what he was about when it came to military tactics. So what to make of Zosimus and his broad charge against Constantine of making cities more, rather than less, vulnerable by neglecting the frontiers?

In fact, if we look at the historical record, then we find it the case that Constantinople was unique among cities in its ability to avoid the sacking and destruction by invading foreign forces that were so often meted out to other more unfortunate urban centres. Between the fifth- and eighth-centuries, the Roman Empire was subject to a catalogue of this kind of terrible city destruction: cities such as Rome fell to the Goths in 410 and the Vandals in 455; Syrian Antioch fell to the invading Persians in 540 and was almost fully destroyed; Jerusalem and Alexandria were also invaded and sacked, as were Ravenna and Carthage. Great and powerful cultural urban centres such as these all showed themselves to be vulnerable: but not Constantinople, which managed to survive and endure, though it was besieged in 626.

Clearly, someone had done something right both in siting and in constructing Constantinople in such a way as to make attack and fall at the hands of an invading force such a difficult task (and naturally, there were many who wanted to accomplish such a thing, since Constantinople was such a glittering prize).

If we look at Constantinople's situation, then we can easily see the first explanation for the city's impressive defensive record. Firstly, the site of Constantinople had the great strategic advantage of being a natural confluence of east and west, making it a very good place from which to get to various different parts of the empire (especially troublesome regions) and of being positioned on a promontory with the natural defences of the sea on either side of the city, so that any land-based army had no choice but to arrive on the narrow promontory. Any army choosing this route of attack would have been very easily seen indeed.

Naturally, the geographical advantages of this location had been noticed well before Constantine's own time, which is why there was already a settlement there by the name of Byzas or Byzantion which had been in existence for over a thousand years.[3] This settlement, the one which Constantine came to, extended roughly to the modern-day Galata Bridge, though it had been improved in various ways by the emperors Caracalla and Septimus Severus. Where in present day Istanbul we find Hagia Sophia, in the city of Byzas as Constantine found it the main civic centre of the town would have been around the agora outside, with the Roman overlay on the Greek foundations of a bath house and a wide street from this centre to the city gates in the west.

Constantine's capitalisation on the geographical advantages offered by the location of the older city of Byzas started with his improvement in the civic amenities. He increased the urban area to around 700 hectares and built for himself a huge palace (which remained the imperial residence for a long while afterwards) and made the road leading to the city gates a more substantial thoroughfare, becoming the main city road.

He then turned his attention to the city defences. As noted, the city was well-defended on most sides by the sea, by virtue of the triangular shaped promontory and extraordinary natural harbour that is the Golden Horn, making land-based attack a difficult feat to pull off. Constantine therefore ensured that this would be made near-impossible indeed by building a set of walls across the land entrance, ensuring that any invading force would find it hard indeed to cross over into Constantinople. It essentially walled Constantinople off from the rest of the Roman Empire; this city defence helped to give Constantinople a superior sense of its own detachment and impregnability that its citizens came to be so proud of in later years.

Indeed, it was a fortunate foresight of Constantine to rebuild the city walls in this way; as we have already heard, the Battle of Adrianople was a catastrophic and embarrassing Roman defeat. After the thorough humiliation of the Romans by the Goths, nothing stood in the way of the Goths; the path was clear to Constantinople since they had managed to do the impossible and overcome the might of the Roman army. The conquering Goths knew a golden opportunity when they saw one, and so of course they made straight for the city; but when they got there and looked at the mighty city walls, they immediately realised that the task of sacking a city which had such strong walls and fortifications was a hopeless one and so they straightaway gave up and withdrew.

Therefore, Constantine's legacy of solid city defence served the city well and long into the future, even protecting Constantinople from the kind of all-round defeat of the Roman army that, in his own lifetime, Constantine would have scarcely been able to believe had he known of it. In fact, so good were Constantine's walls that it wasn't until after the year 400 and the time of Theodosius II that the city walls needed any kind of modification, since the city population had expanded so much (a mark of its success) that the old area marked off by Constantine's walls was proving itself to be too small to accommodate this thriving and expanding urban centre. The walls were therefore moved further out to make even more space for urban expansion, but the fact that the concept of city defence and its necessity was never questioned showed just how good a decision it was of Constantine's in the first place. Indeed, the Theodosian Walls remained Constantinople's major land defence over the next thousand year period of its history, and were its unfailing protection and safeguard against foreign invasion until the fall of Constantinople in 1453. Indeed, Vegetius summarises the key features of good city defence, and it was one of Constantine's many successes that he followed the spirit of this advice:

> Cities and forts are either fortified by nature or by human hand, or by both, which is considered stronger. By 'nature' is meant places which are elevated, precipitous, surrounded by sea, morasses or rivers; by 'hand', fosses and a wall. In places enjoying the safest natural advantages, judgement is required of that of the selector; in a flat place, effort of the founder. We see cities of very great antiquity so built in the midst of spreading plains that in the absence of help from the terrain they were rendered invincible by art and labour.[4]

Zosimus' accusations of incompetence in regards to defensive matters can be partially rebuffed, and Constantinople's reputation as a city built with war in mind and prepared against the eventuality of foreign invasion can stand. Moreover, Constantine's rebuilding and defensive programme had a specific aim in mind: to make the urban fabric suitable for an imperial capital to rival the status of Rome; but of course, also to create the kind of urban fabric that would be necessary to hold the population that would be needed to make Constantinople a city capable of rivalling Rome. A great city needs people to work the infrastructure, and after Constantine's city improvements the population began to grow a great deal more as people were attracted by the new employment opportunities created by virtue of the relocation of the imperial capital. Also, Constantine's efforts to make Byzas into

Constantinople, to relocate the imperial administrative centre, necessitated the creation of a new Senate (though this body was weak and spineless, not a real power centre) and to complement this, a new aristocracy and civil administration, with a whole new set of nomenclature.

But what of his accusation of poor decision making when it came to frontier defence and military strategy? We already know that Zosimus as a source is inclined to be anti-Constantine and pro-Diocletian, since, as a pagan, he disliked Constantine as the first Christian Roman emperor and was a supporter of Diocletian as an emperor responsible for persecution of the Christians and by extension a defender of paganism. Nevertheless, some historical analysis does follow the Zosimus' line, but there is archaeological evidence which suggests that the clear divide Zosimus draws between Diocletian and Constantine is not the fullest or truest picture.

But as other historians and commentators (such as Tomlin) have pointed out, this criticism of Zosimus levied against Constantine regarding the stationing of the army amounts to nothing more than what seems to be a deliberate misunderstanding of the later Roman military reality and strategy. Given the nature of what Constantine was facing at that time (potential threats to the frontiers on many sides) it is understandable that he did not even attempt to cover the entire frontier all at once by stringing out the army along its full extent. This would have only given the frontier a thin defensive coating, rather than the concentrated defence located in a specific region that it actually needed in the event of a real attack. Thus, having a mobile field army that could be fairly quickly and easily mustered and sent to a flash point (assuming that the frontier garrisons could hold off any attack, or at least mitigate its worst extremities, for long enough to allow this to happen) in the event of a conflict was a far better tactic and showed a greater insight into the military reality of the fourth century than Zosimus seems able to allow.

The fact that Constantinople was indeed a city built for war also reminds us of the very pressing need for city defence: it was precisely because the enemies of the Roman Empire were increasingly able to penetrate right to the heart of the power centres – to cities such as Rome, for example – that good city defences were needed. For the citizen of the later Roman Empire, war against the barbarians was no longer something peripheral; something that happened out on the frontiers, waged far away from the urban safety net. Now, the barbarians had increased their organisation and reach and were able to threaten these urban centres, so of course any emperor worthy of holding the office needed to take this new military reality into account. Therefore, Zosimus' accusations increasingly come across as the vain attempt to misread Constantine's decisions as incompetence rather than for what they were: the common-sense reaction to the current reality of the threats he faced and the refusal to be tied to the old ways of doing things that clearly no longer applied.

War and the city: the social dimension

Constantine's positioning of a larger number of forts in a greater number of areas of dense population than there had been before inevitably served to make the army far more visible to the citizenry, and for this reason Zosimus also criticises this decision because (to a civilian and pagan such as Zosimus) it unnecessarily increased tensions between soldier and citizen, to the extent of potentially making the citizen's life intolerable. Zosimus has a point in this regard: no doubt, the men who made up the Roman army in the fourth century were more than capable of abusing their powers, which it seems they certainly did; much to the antagonism of the populaces who had to live close by. For example, Matthew 5.41: 'If anyone forces you to go with him a mile, go with him two miles' and Luke 3.14: 'Then some soldiers asked him "And what should we do?" He replied: "Don't extort money and don't accuse people falsely – be content with your pay"' are both hints at the extent of the common practice of army abuse of position and extortion.

Zosimus blames Constantine for bringing about this kind of civilian/ military tension, but Constantine himself was not unaware of the problem of army misbehaviour and consequently the potential to cause a great deal of friction and unrest. For example, Constantine noticed how the army freely abused their power to requisition horses and oxen for their own trans-portation usage, and attempted to stop this insidious practice by banning soldiers from taking oxen used for ploughing, but it seems that the law carried little weight against an army who were becoming very used to a power balance increasingly skewed towards them. Naturally, this kind of animal requisition was done in a fashion almost designed to cause maxi-mum outrage to the civilian populace: there was a general sense that it was practised entirely for greed, rather than for any genuine military need; the animals in question were rarely returned in good condition (though they were supposed to be), and the military were probably more likely to be heavy-handed and contemptuous rather than polite and self-effacing in their handling of the whole situation. Thus, the army were doing themselves no favours when it came to public relations with the urban populations in which they were increasingly stationed, and worse, were well aware that there was little anyone else could do to stop them, since they were an unquestioned necessity in a Roman Empire of increasing barbarian incursion, creating an urban population well aware of the need for protection against sack and invasion but dissatisfied with the return on their investment in terms of victories achieved.

Therefore, there was little love lost between solider and civilian, though to suggest that all of the citizen population were victims of the soldier's excesses would be to make the reverse mistake of assuming that the people who made up the civilian populations of cities such as Constantinople in the fourth century were not also capable of abusing their power. Detractors such as Zosimus claimed that the army were over-fond of such battle-unfriendly pursuits as wine, women and song; no doubt they were fond of those things, but another way of looking at it is that they were a ripe and ready market for a merchant who could purvey such things and charge accordingly. So despite the many abuses of power foisted on the civilians, the army presence in the city was also a bolster to the local economy, and not just in the kinds of entertainments described above: soldiers were also known to purchase military equipment, kit and related services and in this way would have been a source of income rather than expenditure for the citizenry; a fact of which Zosimus seems unaware.

The art of the siege

Having established that Constantinople was successfully built to withstand a measure of outside attack, and that the new military realities of the era caused some inevitable social repercussions that came from moving the army into the city, we turn to the nature of siege warfare itself. Here is an example of the praxis of this, from Zosimus:

> Vessels arrived at the Hellespont bringing all kinds of goods and an abundant supply of provisions for Constantine's commanders, who then put out with the whole fleet to join in the siege of Byzantium and to blockade the city by sea as well. Licinius' infantry found the mere sight of this fleet unbearable and, taking ship, sailed for Eleus. Constantine devoted himself to the siege [of Licinius] and, building a mound as high as the wall, he placed on it wooden towers overlooking the wall, from which his men could shoot down on the defenders, so that he could safely bring up battering rams and other engines; in this way he was confident of taking the city.[5]

This gives us something of the flavour of how a Roman offensive siege was typically carried out. As we can infer from Zosimus, who narrates this siege as part of the broader outbreaks of hostilities between Constantine and Licinius, sieges were a part and parcel of civil wars. Though in particular on the eastern frontier, Roman armies more routinely undertook sieges against the Persians. (Naturally, the Persians learnt a great deal about siegecraft from this sustained experience, and went on to use Roman siege tactics successfully themselves, which made them fairly unique among Rome's enemies in having the technological capacity and knowhow to successfully wage an offensive siege).

The essence of a good siege, as already discussed, probably most often included that old standby, limitation of the food and water supply to a city or region under attack. This tactic was no doubt used by the Romans frequently, probably more frequently than the written sources attest since it is not so glamorous or exciting a one as those that involve use of the technology of siege warfare. Nevertheless, the Romans certainly had the technological capability to wage an offensive siege based on the assault, rather than that based on the blockade (though this is not to underestimate the level of logistics and forward planning that waging a successful blockade required). However, the Romans understood that blockade was most often 'Plan A', assault being 'Plan B' where that had failed. An assault required the certain confidence in superior firepower, for example, and also reliable siege machinery such as a siege engine. Siege engines could include the *catapulta* (the name changed to *ballista* after the fourth century; previously this had denoted a stone-throwing siege engine, the type of which came to be known as the *onager*) which hurled bolts under torsion. Bolt hurling and stone throwing siege engines each had their own specific advantages, though obviously the aim of both types of machine was to attack both the fortifications and the armies of the besieged. It was also possible to use both types of machine to throw fire; itself a powerful type of assault weapon since this understandably inspired a huge amount of fear among the besieged.

Whereas the Romans could be very confident of their technological prowess as demonstrated in their ability to construct siege engines of the type described above, they could be less confident that their enemies would not also be able to construct a mobile siege tower. Many of Rome's enemies could certainly do this, meaning that they had some capacity to put the boot on the other foot and besiege the Romans, perhaps also utilising techniques such as the blockade themselves. For example, the Goths had their own mobile siege towers which they used in the Balkans around the middle years of the third century. The point of a mobile siege tower was to transport shock troops to weak points on the besieged fortifications, so they could fight hand-to-hand and so force an entrance, or else to give the siege engines a better aspect for an increased range. Besides mobile siege towers, there were also siege mounds or platforms, which gave a better position for launching an attack against either the walls or the besieged defenders. Here is Vegetius describing some of these kinds of siege equipment and the techniques associated with them:

> The ancients called 'vines' what are now called in military and barbarian parlance *cauiae*. The machine is made of light wood, 8 foot wide, 7 foot tall and 16 foot long. The roof is constructed with a double protective covering of boards and hurdles. The sides also are fenced with wicker against penetration by impact of stones and missiles. To avoid combustion from fire-darts the outside is covered with raw and freshly flayed hides and fire-blankets. When a number have been made, they are joined together in a line, and under their shelter besiegers make openings to undermine the foundations of walls in safety.
>
> 'Screens' refers to apse-shaped structures made from wicker, covered with goat's hair mats and hides, and fitted with three wheels, one in the middle and two at the ends, so that they can be moved up in whatever direction you wish, like a wagon. Besiegers can bring them up to walls and sheltering under their cover dislodge all defenders from fortifications by means of arrows, slings and missiles, so as to provide easier opportunity to mount by ladders.
>
> The siege mound is built from earth and timbers against the wall, and from it missiles are shot.[6]

The final technique of a good assault was that of sapping; undermining the defences of a city by underground means or by mines. Like the mobile siege tower, this was a technique that was not unfamiliar to Rome's enemies and was used to force a breach in the besieged fortifications. Here is Vegetius on the modus operandi:

> Another method of assault is subterranean and secret, which they call a 'burrow', after the hares which dig tunnels underground and hide in them. A gang is set to work digging the earth with great labour as in the mines where the industrious Bessi explore veins of gold and silver, and by means of the excavated cave an underground route to the city's destruction is sought. This stratagem is effected by two methods of attack. Either they penetrate beneath the city and, emerging by the burrow at night unbeknown to the townspeople, open the gates to admit a column of their own side who kill the enemy in their own homes taking them unawares; or else when they reach the foundations of the walls, they excavate the largest possible part of them, placing dry timber there and

holding up the collapse of the wall by temporary works. They also add brushwood and other flammable tinder. Then, when the soldiers are ready, fire is introduced to the work and, all the wooden props and boards having burned, the wall suddenly collapses, opening a way for invasive action.[7]

If that is an overview of the ways in which an offensive siege could be carried out, then we can now turn to the obverse. How did the Romans defend a city when they were themselves under siege? It was likely to be the *limitanei* rather than the *comitatenses* who were in the role of defenders of a city under attack, since the *limitanei* were stationed at the frontiers where Rome's enemies might more easily attempt to besiege a Roman fortification or settlement. In order to withstand a siege; to be on the defensive, it was very important indeed to maintain good spirits among the besieged. After all, any mental crack in the determination to withstand a siege and outwit the besiegers could be just as easily exploited by the attacking force as a physical crack in the walls or along the battlements. There were defensive tactics, of course, besides needing to have the logistical insight and cunning to find alternative supply lines into a city in the event of a blockade. For example, a besieged city could find the means to launch an attack of their own at the besiegers, perhaps by using artillery of their own at the attacking force, or by using their own forces to turn the defensive into an offensive opportunity and attack the besiegers while themselves unguarded. Vegetius describes some of the tactics open to a besieged city should the worst happen: the besieging forces manage to force an entrance:

> Countless examples demonstrate that enemies have often been slain to a man after they had invaded a city. This is the certain result, if the citizens hold on to the walls and towers and occupy the higher ground. For then from windows and rooftops people of all ages and both sexes overwhelm the invaders with stones and other kinds of missiles. To avoid this fate, the besiegers frequently open the city gates in order to induce resistance to stop by conceding the chance to escape. For necessity is a desperate kind of courage. In this case there is only one help for the besieged, whether the enemy enters by day or night, and that is to hold the walls and towers, climb the higher ground, and overwhelm the enemy from all sides by fighting it out in the streets and squares.[8]

The intersection between war and the city throws up some interesting points of comparison in this history: the necessity of kitting out a city for the eventuality of siege by definition changes its material fabric; there is an inevitable social tension created when the civilian and military worlds collide, and one that is not necessarily easily resolved; the art of the siege or city warfare itself requires specialised equipment and perhaps also specialist troops; withstanding a siege is also an art of its own, with its own techniques, and even when an invading army do manage to break through the defences, all is not necessarily lost if the home side hold their nerve.

These points of comparison remind us that war has many aspects, as has been a theme of this history: a material one, in the form of military equipment and fortifications; a social one whence are troops recruited; how do they relate to civilian populations, if at all and a technical one what is the praxis or craft of war; what are the tactics or strategies, what is the best psychology of attack or defence.

Chapter 12

Conclusion

The case for Constantine's prowess as a military man and a supreme man of action has been proved. His understanding of the military realities and requirements of battle is evident, his ability to adapt and turn around disadvantage are also shown in this history. His military capabilities created the ground in which Christianity was able to flourish, but more so, his military achievement helped to revolutionise the nature of power in the Roman Empire.

Constantine and North African Christianity
To this end, we turn to examine what was happening to Christianity in North Africa, in particular in Carthage, and how Constantine got involved there, as a demonstration of this. In the early years of the fourth century, North Africa had gained for itself a reputation for being a hotbed of Christian schism, dissent and discord. Besides the tendency towards diversity that can be observed in religious ideas, this particular case was largely a result of the churches in North Africa having suffered particularly in the Great Persecution of Christianity, the last it suffered at the hands of Roman imperial power, in 303–305. In North Africa during the Great Persecution, apparently in a manner which was not copied exactly elsewhere, various state officials interpreted the letter of the law on a sliding scale of severity, according to their own wishes. While some Christians were treated harshly and severely, others who had committed offences in the eyes of the Roman state were given more lenient punishments.

Moreover, there was considerable bad blood stirred up between the remaining Christians as to who had been a quisling traitor and who had remained resolutely faithful to the last. Some Christians had been rather more moderate or flexible than others in their reaction to this last wave of cruel and officially-sponsored persecution. For example, at one extreme, there were those who had given in, in the sense that they had acquiesced to the demands of the Roman state, and had made sacrifice to the emperor and to the traditional deities of Greco-Roman paganism, or worse had informed on their fellow Christians. At the other extreme were all those who had been martyred for their beliefs, who had refused any compromise that was offered nor had made any sort of kow-towing to the demands of Rome. In between these two extremes were those who had made one sort of acquiescence or tried to make one kind of co-operation but not another, and those who had seen it as their duty and done their best to help fellow Christians while they were kept prisoners of conscience or were on their way to their executions. In other words, they had indeed tried to render up to Caesar what they thought was Caesar's, but had also tried to render up to God what they thought was God's.[1]

But the wounds of such cruel persecution are slow to heal: the survivors of the Great Persecution of 303–305 found it very hard in the years following to come to terms with what had happened among them. Accusations back and forth, mistrust, factionalism, schism, and discord were the order of the day in North Africa, and to such an extent and magnitude that the wounds could not be healed by its local members. In fact, by 312/313, they were getting worse and worse rather than better, and what to begin with had been discord mainly centred around Carthage had spilled out and infected the rest of the North African churches, both those in other urban districts besides Carthage and in the more rural areas. The clamour was rising for everyone to take sides; everybody really was shouting: 'which side are you on?' and more-over, prominent clergy, and rich and powerful Christians were using their power and influence where they could, by dragging outsiders into the mess and calling for others to come in and take sides to sort out the confusion. Constantine, as Christian emperor, was obviously one of those high up on the list of desirable candidates the North Africans wanted to involve in an attempt to bring some semblance of order. Understanding that this was not something he was entirely equipped or well-placed to deal with, since it involved going through all the points of conflict on both sides, the human dramas and the doctrinal tensions, he instructed two men on the ground to look closely at what was going on and to try and work out their own con-clusions to all the conflict. These two men were Patricius, the Vicar of the African Diocese, and Anullinus, the Proconsul of Africa.

However, the schism proved too intractable at this stage for Patricius and Anullinus to sort out on their own, and moreover, there was the distinct novelty of actually having a Christian emperor in charge. Rather than having no option but to sort out disputes and conflicts internally, as had always been the case before when Christians saw themselves at odds with and set against secular power, this time round there was so much more on offer. The decisions and pronouncements made by Constantine would carry the weight not only of secular authority but also, and more enticingly, would have something of the flavour of the divine. To my mind, Constantine's involvement in the North African (also known as Donatist, after Donatus who was one of the key players) schism is truly the key moment both in Christian history and in Constantine's own personal history.

Without any of the players, whether large or small, knowing exactly what was going on or what was emerging from this, the North African problem had fundamentally torn open the locus of power in the Roman Empire. The North African schism enacted the idea that the emperor could speak not only with the voice of Caesar but also of God; something that had not been the case before in the same way.

And if that was the case, then a Caesar's word would mean so much the more, and his responsibilities towards that God were also correspondingly immense. Moreover, if the church had the influence and institutional significance to call in secular power into what was essentially a religious difference, then the church was becoming a power broker in its own right that could no longer be ignored or dismissed.

The fact that power was undergoing a recalibration in the Roman Empire in the early part of the fourth century is also shown by Constantine's next major reaction to the difficulties of the North African schism; he used his leverage to invite leading members of the Christian clergy to come to a meeting in Arles in 314 at which it was intended that the North African schism could be sorted out once and for all, where an earlier and smaller Synod had already failed.

Arles was well-positioned to be the location for such an important council of secular power, bishops and clergy. As an urban centre of some importance, conveniently located, a nodal point and something of a transport hub, it was in many ways ideal for this meeting of the factions. The signs certainly looked good; the invitations had been sent in the spring of that year, early enough to give everyone time to prepare and make the journey for the summer. The outcome of the council of Arles was also fairly quick and painless: there were two men vying to be accepted as bishop of Carthage, Donatus and Caecilian, each with their own following and forms of support, and each representing a different side of the fall out of the Great Persecution of 303–305.

Both these men had their chance to speak and to present their case as best they could. This they did, and since Caecilian seemed to have the better argument, presented with more substantiating evidence and to be the better candidate personality wise, the council decided in his favour and

Caecilian was recognised as Bishop of Carthage. The council of Arles, once it had come to this decision, then made good use of its time and sorted through many other pressing issues and concerns of the day, including problems such as when best to celebrate Easter and who should decide the date of this festival, and even more interestingly, what was the role and place of Christianity in the context of the military and within the need for warfare in the Roman Empire as it stood. Clearly, this concern was something that brought together both secular and religious or divine power in the new Christian context.

Finally, the council of Arles was ably presided over by Constantine himself, and he acquitted himself well, considering that he had only been a convert to the faith for two years or so. While he still very much saw the Christian God as his tutelary deity, one whom he owed for his military and secular success, his efforts to acquire the rudiments of Christian learning and education were starting to bear fruit: that he was able to manage the council of Arles without embarrassing himself for his lack of learning or understanding of Christian ideas in front of so many men of learning shows us that whatever the true nature of his conversion experiences, he certainly now took his faith very seriously indeed.

Constantine's conversion is sometimes painted as a definitive, once-and-for all, momentous occasion in the eyes of some historians. It can come across as a watershed moment: before the conversion happened, the Roman Empire was pagan, and after it happened, the Roman Empire was definitively Christian.

In fact, the wholesale conversion to Christianity by the Roman citizenry was slow, and Constantine was part of a broader shift that was taking place, while also being an instigator. What is too often overlooked, however, is that Constantine's conversion to Christianity was most likely precipitated by events that took place in a battlefield context, has only been recorded and given meaning because of his military success and victory (where would Christianity be if Constantine had not been such a successful general?), and as an urban social phenomenon was entirely sustained by, and dependent on, the backbone of the Roman Empire, the competence, success and strategy of the Roman army.

Notes

Chapter One – Introduction
1. Cameron and Hall, 1999, 3.
2. *VC* 1.10.1.
3. *VC* 1.10.2.
4. *VC* 1.10.3.
5. *VC* 1.10.2; 1.10.3.
6. It is an interesting piece of etymology that the Latin word for military triumph: *virtus* (whence the English 'virtue') is related to the Latin word for man: *vir*, thus linking military prowess, bravery, moral excellence and manliness in one fell swoop.
7. Nixon and Rodgers, 1994, 33–35.
8. *Hist.* 1.57.
9. *Hist.* 1.1.2.
10. The issue of Zosimus' philosophical leanings is still one of academic debate and historiographical interest. To explain his fatalism, some have laid the charge of neoplatonism at the feet of Zosimus, though the philosopher A H Armstrong lays that one to rest, in the following footnote to be found in the commentary on the *Nea Historia*: 'To speak safely of Neo-Platonism in Zosimus we would need evidence of "the One of Good beyond being and thought, sharply distinguished from *Nous*, divine hexads, a tendency to arrange spiritual beings in triads, an unconscious *physis* distinct from higher cosmic soul, a rejection of the "artisan" concept of creation generally held by Jews and Christians, strange and original ideas about human personality and consciousness, etc" ': Ridley, 2006, 135.
11. *VC* 1.13.1.
12. Beard, North and Price 1, 1998, 286: 'Many of the new cults [including Mithraism] proclaimed the superiority of one single supreme deity'.

13. It is Ambrose who refers to Helena in this way, in the *oratio de obitu Theodosiani 42*, in the *Patrologiae cursus completus, series Latina* 16: 1463.
14. *Origo* 1.2.
15. Lieu and Montserrat, 1998, 78–79.
16. *Origo* 2.2.
17. *Hist* 2.9.2.
18. Harnack, 1908, 2.139.
19. Origen, *Contra Celsus*, 3.52.
20. Luke 17:20–21.
21. For example Ramsay MacMullen (1984, 39) who in a discussion of the spread of Christianity in the Roman Empire recognises that: 'women, except at the absolute top of society, did in fact enjoy far less access to advanced education and wide reading than men ... so their capacity for critical discrimination would be less well developed.' While it is certainly true that few women in the Roman Empire would have been able to hold their own against a well-educated man who had access to training in rhetoric, literature and the law (among other things), the fact of women's lower educational attainment in the Roman Empire is not to my mind the salient reason behind women's greater enthusiasm for Christianity.
22. Although the teaching of Galatians 3:28 'So there is no difference between Jews and Gentiles; between slaves and free men, between men and women; you are all one in union with Christ Jesus' is attributed to Saint Paul, he also instructs early Church communities in 1 Corinthians 11:3: 'But I want you to understand that Christ is supreme over every man, the husband is supreme over his wife, and God is supreme over Christ.' Moreover: 'Nor was man created for woman's sake, but woman was created for man's sake.' (1 Corinthians 11:9). This is one of the splits in the Pauline discourse, and it seems that he struggles with aligning one interpretation of Jesus' message with a deeply ingrained Greco-Roman misogyny. As Fiorenza, 1983, xiii–xxv suggests, there is considerable evidence that women's real and substantial contribution to early Christianity and the fact of their discipleship has been overlooked by the male authors of the Gospel narrative, who have filtered this history through a more acceptable contemporary patriarchy. In other words, the New Testament has been redacted.
23. Bauckham, 2002, 295: 'The women as authoritative witnesses in the Early Church.'
24. E.g., 1 Timothy 2:12 on the necessity for women's silence in the Church. Despite this and a few other comments which have been read as prohibiting women intellectual freedom and barring them from holding

authority over men, the narrative of Acts is full of clues showing that (just as in the Gospel narratives) women were drawn both to Jesus and to Christianity in their numbers, and like men were attracted to a variety of roles suitable to their talents within that early Christian culture. For example, at Acts 18:26 we learn that: 'He [Apollos, a Jewish convert] began to speak boldly in the synagogue. When Priscilla and Aquila heard him, they took him home with them and explained to him more correctly the Way of God.' Priscilla and Aquila were a married couple, but what is of note here is that the woman's name comes first. This name ordering suggests that Priscilla may have taken precedence in terms of her competence in evangelising and teaching, which is what she and her husband Aquila are shown doing here.

25. Though the extent to which this remained the case by Helena's own time of the late-third and early-fourth centuries is another matter. It is certainly the case that Christianity acquired a male–dominated hierarchy and a more misogynist strand of interpretation that was in line with the time. This process was already underway in the second century AD: Lane Fox, 1987, 308–11.

26. *Paneg.* 6 (7) 3.4.

27. Tertullian, a prolific Christian apologist, is often quoted on the productive and fertile effect that violent and public persecution of the Roman type had on nascent Christianity, contrary to the one intended: 'the blood of the martyrs is seed'. *Apologeticum* 50.

28. This diverse religious/cultural mix has been memorably described as: 'a world full of Gods' in his same-titled book on religion in the Roman Empire: Hopkins, 1999.

29. Isis-worship really grabbed the Roman imagination, though its more private, cultic and initiate–only dimension also appealed for other reasons, as Apuleius' allegorical novel on initiation into the mysteries of Isis, *The Golden Ass*, demonstrates.

30. Roth, 2009, 251: a mosaic dated to the third or fourth century shows two Roman soldiers, one of whom has a *crux gammata* on his tunic. This probably indicates that as a soldier he has some adherence to Mithras, but the very same symbol also came to be used in a more specifically Christian context, showing us the give-and-take that was going on between pagan and Christian culture in this period. The military, as a significant section of Roman society at large, were no less a part of this cultural shift.

Chapter 2 – The Army: The Social Context

1. In some instances where the right conditions are met, the pidgin has enough traction to become a native language to the children born of

such parents, and may even thereby supersede the original languages in prestige, thus becoming a new standard, or creole, named for the Portuguese and Spanish colonisation of parts of Africa, the West Indies and South America where we have the world's paramount example of this process taking place.

2. Maurice, *Strategikon* 1.2.
3. Though the Greek designation for 'mercenary' is not itself unproblematic (for a discussion on this: Trundle, 2004, 10–21). *Misthotoi* is in fact a diminutive with derogatory connotation, derived from the Greek *misthos* (pay; wage) and could be translated as something like 'hirelings' rather than the more standard or neutral Greek term for mercenary: *misthophoroi* (lit: 'wage bearers').

   However, the first use of the Latin term *foederati* (usually trans: federates) as meaning Frankish troops who fought for Rome in return for farmland along depopulated stretches of the Rhine after their period of service is recorded under the emperor Julian in the middle of the fourth century, rather than under Constantine himself.

4. Southern, 2001, 270.
5. Veg., *Mil.* 1.2.
6. Veg., *Mil.* 1.3.
7. Veg., *Mil.* 1.4.

Chapter 3 – The Rise of Constantine: Army, Tetrarchy and Frontiers

1. Cary and Scullard, 1975, 518.
2. This first stage of this new system could more exactly be referred to as 'diarchy', (following the derivation of tetrarchy; Greek *duo*: two) or rule by two individuals.
3. Lenski, 2006, 326.
4. Cary and Scullard, 1975, 520.
5. Grant, 1985, 212.
6. Cary and Scullard, 1975, 522.
7. Lenski, 2006, 326–7.
8. Southern, 2001, 272.
9. *CTh.* 7.20.4.
10. The *Notitia Dignitatum* (9.4–8; 11.4–10) records there being seven *scholae* in the east and five *scholae* in the west.
11. *CTh.* 7.20.4.
12. MacMullen, 1969, 42–44.
13. *Hist.* 2.34.
14. Southern, 2001, 273.

15. Lenski, 2006, 327.
16. Brennan, 1998, 238–44.
17. Lenski, 2006, 327.
18. Goldsworthy, 2000, 124–5; John Lydus, *De Mens* 1.27; Treadgold, 1995, 43–64; Lenski, 2006, 332. Jones, 1964 agrees with the figure of 600,000.
19. Tacitus, *Annals* 4.5.
20. Mann, 1977, 11–15; Lenski, 2006, 330.
21. *Hist.* 2.33.3.
22. Lenski, 2006, 331.
23. Veg., *Mil.* 3.6.
24. Elton, 1996, 107.
25. Bishop and Coulston, 2006, 202.
26. Roth, 2009, 234; 285.
27. English, 2009a.
28. Goldsworthy, 2003, 120ff.
29. *CTh.* 7.4.6.
30. Veg., *Mil.* 3.3.
31. Southern, 2001, 274–5.
32. Dodgeon and Lieu, 1991, 34–67.
33. Southern, 2001, 278–9.

Chapter 4 – Turin and Verona
1. *Const. Porph.*, B.1–19, trans Haldon (1990).
2. Barnes, 1981, 39.
3. *DMP* 36.1.
4. Odahl, 2004, 102.
5. *Paneg..* 12.5.1–2.
6. *Hist.* 2.1.1.
7. *Paneg.* 4.22.4.
8. *Paneg.* 4.23.4.
9. *Paneg.* 4.24.2.
10. *Paneg.* 12.6.2.
11. *Paneg.* 12.6.2–3.
12. *Paneg.* 12.6.3.
13. *Paneg.* 4.24.2.
14. *Paneg.* 4.24.3–4.
15. *Paneg.* 12.6.6.
16. *Paneg.* 12.6.6. Cf. Odahl, 2004, 102.
17. *Paneg.* 12.7.5–8.
18. *Paneg.* 4.25.1–2.
19. *Paneg.* 12.8.2.

20. Odahl, 2004, 103.
21. *Paneg.* 12.8.4.
22. *Paneg.* 12.9.1.
23. *Paneg.* 12.9.3.
24. *Paneg.* 12.10.1–2.
25. Grant, 1993, 37.

Chapter 5 – The Milvian Bridge
1. Grant, 1993, 37.
2. *VC* 1.27.1.
3. *VC* 1.27.3.
4. *VC* 1.28.1.
5. *VC* 1.28.2.
6. *VC* 1.29.
7. *VC* 1.31.1–3.
8. *VC* 1.30.
9. *VC* 1.32.2–3.
10. Although to be fair to Constantine's own intellectual capacity, he was later educated and instructed in his new-found Christian faith both by his mother Helena and the noted Christian writer and theologian Lactantius, who both came to Constantine in Trier in 313. Moreover, Constantine clearly recognised the importance of rigorous educational standards. Evidence of his high accord in this regard is made clear by the fact that he then desired the respected and talented Lactantius to work as tutor to his son Crispus in his court at Trier, to teach him Latin. The effect of having the great Christian man of letters at the imperial court no doubt had a hugely important impact on the culture of thinking and learning that would have extended beyond Crispus to include other members of the imperial family, such as Helena and, of course, Constantine himself.
11. Odahl, 2004, 106.
12. *Religio* is the Latin term generally employed to refer to a religious practice considered truly 'Roman': pious, moral and manly, whereas *superstitio* is the more pejorative term used to refer to anybody else's religious practice: foreign, effeminate and immoral. In reality, there never was such a clear boundary between what was *religio* and what was *superstitio*; it is only Eusebius' Christian bias that leads him to think of Maxentius' religious practice as *superstitio* whereas his is *religio*. For a discussion on this, see: Beard, North and Price 2, 1998, and for Eusebius on the evils of Maxentius: *VC* 1.33.1–1.36.2.

13. *Hist.* 2.29.3–4.
14. *VC* 1.32.3.
15. Grant, 1993, 38.
16. *Paneg.* 12.16.3–4.
17. *Hist.* 2.16.1–3.
18. *Hist.* 2.16.4.
19. *Hist.* 2.17.1–2.

Chapter 6 – Campus Ergenus

1. *VC* 1.39.2.
2. *VC* 1.39.3.
3. Odahl, 2004, 111.
4. *VC* 1.39.3.
5. *VC* 1.32.42.
6. Odahl, 2004, 116.
7. *DMP* 45.1.
8. Odahl, 2004, 119.
9. Barnes, 1981, 63.
10. *DMP* 45.2ff.
11. So called *Campus Ergenus* by Odahl, 2004, 120.
12. *DMP* 46.1ff.
13. Barnes, 1981, 63.
14. *DMP* 46.1ff.
15. Barnes, 1981, 63.
16. Barnes, 1981, 63.

Chapter 7 – War with Licinius: Cibalae and Campus Ardiensis

1. Odahl, 2004, 121.
2. *Paneg.* 12.21–22.
3. Odahl, 2004, 164.
4. Barnes, 1981, 66.
5. *Hist.* 2.18.1–2. (Cf Barnes, 1981, 67. Pohnsander, 1995).
6. *VC* 2.2.3.
7. *VC* 2.3.1.
8. *VC* 2.5.2–4.
9. *Hist.* 2.18.3–5.
10. *Hist* 2.18.3–4.
11. Odahl, 2004, 164.
12. Odahl, 2004, 165 argues for Philippi, *contra* Barnes, 1981, 67 and Grant, 1993, 42–43 who argue for Philippopolis.
13. Lenski, 2006, 74.

14. Odahl, 2004, 164.
15. Barnes, 1981, 67.
16. *VC* 2.7.1.
17. Barnes, 1981, 67.
18. Barnes, 1981, 67.

Chapter 8 – Resumption of War: Adrianople, Byzantium and Chrysopolis

1. *VC* 2.20.2 – 21.1.
2. Odahl, 2004, 167.
3. Curran, 2000, 63–5; Lenski, 2006, 75; De Decker, 1968.
4. Lenski, 2006, 75.
5. *VC* 4.3.
6. Barnes, 1981, 69.
7. *VC* 1.55.1–2.
8. Barnes, 1981, 70.
9. *Hist.* 2.21.1–3.
10. Lenski, 2006, 75.
11. Lenski, 2006, 75.
12. *Hist.* 2.22
13. *Hist.* 2.23.3.
14. *Hist.* 2.22.1–2.
15. *Origo* 5.23–28; *Hist.* 2.22–28; cf. Pears, 1909, 3ff; Barnes, 1981, 76ff.
16. *VC* 2.15.
17. *Origo* 5.23.
18. Barnes, 1981, 76.
19. Odahl, 2004, 178.
20. *Hist.* 2.23.4–6.
21. *Hist.* 2.23–25; *Origo* 5.24–25. The best modern account of the battle is Odahl, 2004: he demonstrates an understanding of strategy and tactics that many other modern authors, on this occasion, do not.
22. Odahl, 2004, 178.
23. English, 2009b, 85–103.
24. Odahl, 2004, 179–80.
25. Odahl, 2004, 180.
26. *Hist.* 2.26.1.
27. Lenski, 2006, 76.
28. *Hist.* 2.26.3.
29. *Origo* 5.27–29; *Hist.* 2.26–28; cf. Odahl, 2004, 181.
30. *VC* 2.19.
31. *Hist.* 2.29.1.

Chapter 9 – Imperial Reorganisation and the Final Campaigns

1. Lenski, 2006, 77.
2. Cities like: Trier, Aquileia, Sirmium, Nicomedia, Antioch and Thessaloniki had all enjoyed periods of imperial favour.
3. Lenski, 2006, 77.
4. Southern, 2001, 178.
5. *CAH* Vol. XIII, 7:
6. Lenski, 2006, 78: *augustae* is the feminine plural.
7. *Hist.* 2.29.2.
8. *Hist.* 2.29.3–4.
9. Grant, 1993, 59.
10. Stephenson, 2009, 224–5: 'The bridge between Oescus and Sucidava on the Danube, almost 2.5 km in length, was built towards the end of Constantine's reign in AD 328.' (Austin and Rankov, 1995, 236)
11. Stephenson, 2009, 225.
12. Grant, 1993, 59.
13. Grant, 1993, 62.
14. Odahl, 2004, 253.
15. Stephenson, 2009, 226.
16. Stephenson, 2009, 226.
17. *VC* 3, cited in Grant, 1993, 64.
18. *Origo Constantini* 6.15: *sic cum his pace firmata in Sarmatas versus est, qui dubiae fidei probantur.* Trans: 'Once peace with the Goths had in this way been assured, Constantine turned against the Sarmatians, who were proving themselves to be of dubious loyalty.'
19. Lenski, 2006, 81.
20. *VC* 3 cited in Grant, 1993, 64.
21. *Origo* 32; *VC* 4.5.1–2; Grant, 1993, 63.
22. Stephenson, 2009, 227.
23. *VC* 1.8.2–4, 2.28.2–29.1, 4.9.1, 4.50.1; cf. Lenski, 2006, 81.
24. *VC* 4.9.1–13.1; Lenski, 2006, 81.
25. Lenski, 2006, 81.
26. Grant, 1993, 78; Lenski, 2006, 82.

Chapter 10 – The Future of the Roman Empire

1. *VC* 4.66.1–66.2.
2. *VC* 4.67.1–67.3.
3. *cesset superstitio, sacrificiorum aboleatur insania*: let superstition cease, let the insanity of sacrifice be abolished. *CTh.* 16.10.2.
4. For example Matthew 5:9: 'blessed are the peacemakers, for they will be called children of God.'

5. *VC* 4.18.1.
6. MacMullen, 1984, 47.
7. *VC* 4.18.3.
8. Roth, 2009, 239–240.
9. For example: 'Constantine the Augustus at the request of Sylvester the Bishop constructed the Basilica for the Blessed Peter the Apostle.' *Liber Pontificalis* 34.16.
10. Barbero, 2007.
11. *Amm. Marc.* 31.13.

Chapter 11 – Constantinople: War and the City

1. *Chronicon Paschale* (284–628 AD) 1, AD 328.
2. *Hist.* 2.34.
3. Byzas is a character in Greek mythology after whom the city was thought to have been named.
4. Veg. *Mil.* 4.1.
5. *Hist.* 2.24.3–2.25.1.
6. Veg. *Mil.* 4.15.
7. Veg. *Mil.* 4.24.
8. Veg. *Mil.* 4.25.

Chapter 12 Conclusion

1. Matthew 22:21. This saying attributed to Jesus has become a standard touchstone for Christians in their understanding of the relationship between secular and heavenly authority.

Bibliography

Abbreviations

Ammianus Marcellinus *The Later Roman Empire (AD 354–378): Amm. Marc.*
Anonymus Valesianus *The Origin of Constantine (Origo Constantini)*: *Origo*
Eusebius *History of the Church (Historia Ecclesia)*: *HE*
Eusebius *Life of Constantine (Vita Constantini)*: *VC*
Lactantius *On the death of the Martyrs (De Morte Persecutorum)*: *DMP*
The Latin Panegyrics *Panegyrici Latini*: *Paneg*
Vegetius *Epitome of Military Science (Epitome Rei Militaris)*: *Mil*
Zosimus *New History (Historia Nova)*: *Hist*

Primary Sources

Cameron, A and Hall, S G (trans.), *Eusebius: Life of Constantine* (Oxford, 1999)

Hamilton, W (trans) *Ammianus Marcellinus: The Later Roman Empire (AD 354–378)* (Penguin, 1986)

Milner, N P (trans) *Vegetius: Epitome of Military Science, Translated Texts for Historians Vol 16 Second Revised Edition* (Liverpool University Press, 1996)

Nixon, C E V and Rodgers, B S *In Praise of Later Roman Emperors: The Panegyrici Latini: Introduction, Translation and Historical Commentary with the Latin text of R. A. B. Mynors* (University of California Press, 1994)

Ridley, R T *Zosimus: New History A Translation with Commentary* (Australian Association for Byzantine Studies, 2006)

Chronicon Paschale *(284–628 AD)*

Theodosian Code *(Codex Theodosia)*: *CTh*

Notitia Dignitatum

Maurice *Strategikon*

Tacitus *Annals*

Secondary sources

Alexander, S S 'Studies in Constantinian Church Architecture', *RAC*, Vol.47 (1971), pp. 281–330; ibid., Vol. 49 (1973), pp. 33–44

Alföldi, A *The Conversion of Constantine and Pagan Rome* (Trans. Harold Mattingly: Oxford 1998)

Austin, N J E and Rankov, N B *Exploratio: Military and political intelligence in the Roman world from the second Punic War to the Battle of Adrianople* (Routledge, 1995)

Barbero, A *The Day of the Barbarians* (London 2007)

Beard, M and North, J (eds.) *Pagan Priests: Religion and Power in the Ancient World* (London 1990)

Beard, M, North, J, and Price, S *Religions of Rome* (Vol. I: A History; Vol. II: A Sourcebook) (Cambridge 1998)

Barnes, T D 'The Victories of Constantine the Great', *ZPE* 20, 1976, 149–55

Barnes, T D *Constantine and Eusebius* (London 1981)

Bauckham, R *Gospel Women: Studies of the Named Women in the Gospels* (London 2002)

Baynes, N H *Constantine the Great and the Christian Church* (New York 1975)

Birley, E *The Roman Army* (Amsterdam 1988)

Bishop, M C and Coulston, J C N *Roman Military Equipment From the Punic Wars to the Fall of Rome, 2nd ed.* (London 2006)

Le Bohec, Y *The Imperial Roman Army* (London 1994)

Bowman, A K, Cameron, A, and Garnsey, P (eds.) *The Cambridge Ancient History, Vol XII, The Crisis of Empire, A.D. 193–337* (Second edition: Cambridge 2005)

Brennan, P, 'Divide and Fall: The Separation of Legionary Cavalry and the Fragmentation of the Roman Empire', in *Ancient History in a Modern University: Proceedings of a Colloquium Held at Macquarie University, 8–13 July 1993*, Vol. 2, pp. 238–44, ed. T. W. Hillard (Grand Rapids, Michigan 1998)

Brewer, R J (ed) *Roman Fortresses And Their Legions* (London 2000)

Brown, P *The World of Late Antiquity: A.D. 150–750* (London 1971)

Cameron, A and Garnsey, P (eds.) *The Cambridge Ancient History, Vol XIII, The Late Empire, A.D. 337–425* (Second edition: Cambridge 1998)

Cameron, A and Hall, S G *Eusebius' Life of Constantine* (Oxford 1999)

Cameron, A *Constantine and the Peace of the Church* (Cambridge 2005)

Campbell, B *The Roman Army 31 BC–AD 337* (London 1994)

Campbell, B *Greek and Roman Military Writers: Selected Readings* (London 2004)

Campbell, J *The Emperor and the Roman Army* (Oxford 1984)

Carman, J and Harding, A (ed's.) *Ancient Warfare* (Stroud, Gloucestershire 1999)

Carmody, D L *Biblical Women: Contemporary Reflections on Scriptural Texts* (London 1988)

Cary, M and Scullard, H H *A History of Rome* (London 1975)

Cheesman, G *The Auxilia of the Roman Imperial Army* (Oxford 1914)

Cherry, D *The Roman World: A Sourcebook* (Oxford 2001)

Cowan, R *Roman Battle Tactics: 103 BC-AD 313* (Oxford 2007)

Curran, J *Pagan City and Christian Capital: Rome in the Fourth Century* (Oxford 2000)

De Decker, D 'La Politique Religieuse de Maxence', *Byzantion* 38, 1968, 472–562

Deen, E *All of the Women of the Bible* (San Francisco 1988)

Dixon, K and Southern, P *Roman Cavalry* (London 1992)

Dodgeon, MH and Lieu, S N C *The Roman Eastern Frontier and the Persian Wars (AD 226–363)* (London 1991)

Downey, G *The Late Roman Empire* (New York 1964)

Drake, H A *Constantine and the Bishops: The Politics of Intolerance* (Baltimore 2000)

Dyson, S L *The Creation of the Roman Frontier* (Guildford 1985)

Ehrhardt, C 'Monumental Evidence for the Date of Constantine's First War Against Licinius', *AncW* 23.2, 1992, 87–94

Elliott, T G *The Christianity of Constantine the Great* (Scranton Pasadena 1996)

Elton, H *Warfare in Roman Europe, AD 350–425* (Oxford 1996)

English, S *The Army of Alexander the Great* (Barnsley 2009a)

English, S *The Sieges of Alexander the Great* (Barnsley 2009b)

Ferris, I M *Enemies of Rome: Barbarians Through Roman Eyes* (Stroud, Gloucestershire 2000)

Fiorenza, E S *In Memory of Her: A Feminist Theological Reconstruction of Christian Origins* (London 1983)

Fowden, G *Empire to Commonwealth: Consequences of Monotheism in Late Antiquity* (Princeton 1993)

Freeman, C *AD 381: Heretics, Pagans and the Christian State* (London 2008)

Frend, W H C *The Donatist Church* (3rd Edition: Oxford 1986)

Gilliver, C M *The Roman Art of War* (Stroud, Gloucestershire 1999)

Goldsworthy, A *Roman Warfare* (London 2000)

Goldsworthy, A *The Complete Roman Army* (London 2003)

Grant, M *The Emperor Constantine* (London 1993)

Grant, M *The Roman Emperors: A Biographical Guide to Imperial Rome 31 BC–AD 476* (London 1985)

Grant, M *The Emperor Constantine* (London 1993)

Grimbly, S (ed.) *Encyclopedia of the Ancient World* (London, 2000)

Haldon, J F *Three Treatises on Imperial Military Expeditions* (Vienna, 1990)

Hanson, V D *Why the West Was Won* (London 2001)

Hanson, V D (ed.) *The Makers of Ancient Strategy: From the Persian Wars to the Fall of Rome* (Oxford 2010)

Harris, W V *War and Imperialism in Republican Rome* (Oxford 1979)

Harris, J *Constantinople: Capital of Byzantium* (London, 2007)

Harnack, A *The Mission and Expansion of Christianity in the First Three Centuries* (Trans. J Moffat: 2 vols. New York 1908)

Hartley, E *Constantine the Great: York's Roman Emperor* (London 2004)

Hearsey, J E N *City of Constantinople* (London 1963)

Helgeland, J 'Christians and the Roman Army A.D. 173–337', *CH* 43, 1974, 149–63

Hopkins, K *A World Full Of Gods: Pagans, Jews and Christians in the Roman Empire* (London 1999)

Jones, A M H *The Later Roman Empire* (London 1964)

Jones, T and Ereira, A *Barbarians: An Alternative Roman History* (London 2006)

Julian, T *Constantine, Christianity and Constantinople* (Oxford 2005)

Jensen, R M *The Cambridge History of Christianity: Vol. 1, Origins of Constantine* (Cambridge 2006)

Keppie, L *The Making of the Roman Army: From Republic to Empire* (New York 1984)

Kirsch, J *God Against the Gods: The History of the War Between Monotheism and Polytheism* (New York 2004)

Krautheimer, R *Early Christian and Byzantine Architecture* (4th Edition: New Haven 1986)

Lane Fox, R *Pagans and Christians* (New York 1987)

Lee, A D *War in Late Antiquity: A Social History* (Oxford 2007)

Lenski, N *The Cambridge Companion to the Age of Constantine* (Cambridge 2006)

Lieu, S N C and Montserrat, D *Constantine: History, Historiography and Legend* (London 1998)

Luttwak, E N *The Grand Strategy of the Roman Empire* (Baltimore 1976)

Maas, M *Readings In Late Antiquity: A Sourcebook* (London 2000)

Maclagan, M *The City of Constantinople* (London 1968)

Mango, C (ed.) *The Oxford History of Byzantium* (Oxford 2002)

Mango, C *Byzantium: The Empire of the New Rome* (London 1980)

Mango, C *Studies on Constantinople* (Aldershot 1993)

MacMullen, R 'Constantine and the Miraculous', *GRBS* 9, 1968, 81–96

MacMullen, R *Constantine* (London 1969)

MacMullen, R *Christianizing the Roman Empire, A.D. 100–400* (London 1984)

Mann, J C '*Duces* and *Comites* in the Fourth Century', in *The Saxon Shore*, Johnston, D E (ed.) (London 1977)

Mickelsen, A (ed.) *Women, Authority and the Bible* (Illinois 1986)

Mitchell, S *A History of the Later Roman Empire AD 284–641: The Transformation of the Ancient World* (Oxford 2007)

Magdalino, P. *Studies on the History and Topography of Byzantine Constantinople* (Aldershot, 2007)

Odahl, C M *Constantine and the Christian Empire* (New York, 2004)

Odahl, C M *Constantine and the Christian Empire* (London 2004)

Pears, E 'The Campaign Against Paganism, AD 324', *English Historical Review* 24, 1909, 1–17

Peddie, J *The Roman War Machine* (Stroud, Gloucestershire 1994)

Pohlsander, H A *Helena: Empress and Saint* (Chicago 1995)

Pohlsander, H A *The Emperor Constantine* (London 1996)

Pohlsander, H A *The Emperor Constantine* (Second Edition, London 2004)

Potter, D S *The Roman Empire At Bay: AD 180–395* (Oxford 2004)

Rich, J and Shipley, G *War and Society in the Roman World* (London 1993)

Rich, J (ed) *The City in Late Antiquity: Leicester-Nottingham Studies in Ancient Society Vol 3* (London 1996)

Roth, J P *Roman Warfare* (Cambridge 2009)

Sabin, P, Van Wees, H, and Whitby, M *The Cambridge History of Greek and Roman Warfare* (Cambridge 2007)

Saddington, D *The Development of the Roman Auxiliary Forces from Caesar to Vespasian* (Harare 1982)

Sheriman, N *Stoic Warriors: The Ancient Philosophy Behind the Military Mind* (Oxford 2005)

Simkins, M *The Roman Army from Hadrian to Constantine* (London 1979)

Southern, P *The Roman Empire from Severus to Constantine* (London 2001)

Southern, P and Dixon, K R *The Later Roman Army* (London 1996)

Steed, B L *Piercing the Fog of War: Recognizing Change on the Battlefield* (Minneapolis, Minnesota 2009)

Stephenson, P *Constantine: Unconquered Emperor, Christian Victor* (London 2009)

Sulimirski, T *The Sarmatians* (London 1970)

Syme, R *The Roman Revolution* (Oxford 1952)

Tomlinson, R *From Mycenae to Constantinople: The Evolution of the Ancient City* (London, 1992)

Treadgold, W *Byzantium and its Army, 284–1081* (Stanford 1995)

Trundle, M *Greek Mercenaries: From the Late Archaic Period to Alexander* (Oxford, 2004)

Tilley, M A *The Bible in Christian North Africa: The Donatist World* (Minneapolis, Minnesota 1997)

Williams, S *Diocletian and the Roman Recovery* (London 1985)

Index